PRAYING FOR

the GUILT-FREE Prayer Journal FOR MOMS

GUILT

JEANNIE St JOHN TAYLOR

ILLUSTRATIONS BY PHILLIP RODGERS

THE GUILT-FREE PRAYER JOURNAL FOR MOMS
©2003, by Jeannie St. John Taylor
Published by AMG Publishers

ISBN: 0-89957-138-7

Interior and cover art by Phillip Rodgers, Chattanooga, TN

Interior design and typesetting by Rick Steele

Edited and Proofread by Jonathan Wright, Dan Penwell, and Rick Steele

Printed in Canada
07 06 05 04 03 –T– 5 4 3 2 1

To Petey (LaVon) Prater

You have taught me so much about prayer!

CONTENTS

ACKNOWLEDGMENTS

It would not be possible for me to write a book without lots of help. That's why I sigh over the inadequacy of the English language at a time like this. I need stronger words than thanks and gratitude to tell how much I appreciate everyone who is a part of this book. My special thanks to:

- The friends who lifted me up in prayer as I wrote. A few committed to pray daily; others prayed whenever I requested special prayer support. Thank you to Gloria Penwell, Ann Varnum, Cherie Norman, Marilyn Dale, Linda Moore, Peggy Wood, Amanda Eggert, Petey Prater, Susan Standley, Barbara Martin, Bette Nordberg, Nancy Russell, Helen Haidle, Nancy Taylor, Joan Burdon, Jodi Kinzinger, Carol Klein, Carol Gilbert, Kirsten Norgaard, Laurel Starr, and Tori Taylor. A special thank-you to my parents, Gladys and Clare St. John, for their prayers.

- My friend, prayer partner, and writing buddy for about twenty years, Barbara Martin, who critiqued every chapter before I sent the manuscript to my publisher. She keeps me from saying things she knows I don't mean.

- Dan Penwell, who not only is a great editor who skillfully smoothes and rearranges my words but also is a close friend whose character I admire. Though I can't attest to this personally, I hear he plays a mean game of ping-pong.

- My son, Ty Taylor, who shares many of his amazing ideas with me and gave me permission to write about one in this book. Also to my daughter, Tori, who was an inspiration for parts of the book.

- Philip Rogers, a wonderful artist and designer. I am thrilled to have his delightful illustrations in the interior of this book.

- My husband, Ray, and son Tevin, who didn't make me help with the remodeling and never complained when they had to scrounge their own dinners.

- My wonderful AMG family. I love every one of them.

- My copy editor, Jonathan Wright, who is a wonderful wordsmith. I praise God for your abilities.

- My editor and typesetter, Rick Steele, who corrected all the jots and tittles that never even entered by mind.

- And Ron Mehl, my late pastor. He showed Jesus' love to so many, giving me an example to follow.

INTRODUCTION

Why Should You Pray for Your Children?

Because when you pray in Jesus' name, you tap into a power that outshines Harry Potter's puny magic. When you pray, the King of all the countless kings who have ever lived stops to listen. And he longs to grant the desires of your heart.

Both of my grandmothers knew that and spent much time in prayer. At least one of them began praying for me before my birth and continued interceding for me until the day she died. My mother and father both inherited that deep love for prayer. They prayed as they raised me. They still pray together for my family daily—even though I've been gone from their home for forty years and my own three children are grown. Like my grandmother and parents, I hold prayer in high esteem. One of my highest goals is to pray without ceasing.

My twenty-three-year-old daughter also considers prayer a priority in her life and has told me several times that she thinks of herself as a woman of prayer. Every time I hear her pray, I'm awed. Her powerful, spirit-directed words leave me breathless.

Since I value prayer, and my daughter prays, do you assume that I taught her how to pray? Well, I didn't. Frankly, I don't remember how much we did or did not pray together, and neither does she. I know we prayed before meals and at bedtime. I remember that from a very early age she started asking me to pray for her to do her best in sporting events and on tests. But since I usually prayed silently, I don't know if she was even aware of how frequently I prayed.

Nevertheless, I believe all the hours of prayer I poured into her had something to do with the way she prays now. Because I asked the Lord to teach her to pray, he provided a high school youth group who once welcomed in the New Year by spending four hours on their knees. When she traveled to England for a semester, I asked the Lord to help her grow spiritually. He provided an on-fire-for-the-Lord church next door to her flat at Oxford. I prayed for her to choose good friends. God provided close associates who encourage her in the Lord.

I'm convinced that as we ask God to give our children the character traits he values, he answers our prayers by gradually shaping them into people he can use, godly people who value prayer. As we pray for them, he himself teaches them to pray.

And if they learn to depend on God through prayer, their lives will be successful. What greater gift could we give them?

How to Use This Journal

The writings in this book will guide you into effective ways to pray for your children. As you read the inspirational writings, pray the scripture-prayers, and write out your specific requests, God will make you more and more sensitive to the spiritual and emotional needs of your children. He'll prompt you to pray for them and will then open your eyes to the times he answers your prayers. If you listen carefully, he may even reveal why he feels it necessary to say no to you occasionally.

As you record God's responses in the "Watching for Answers" section, you'll be creating a permanent record of your children's lives. Someday your children will read your journal and be encouraged as they see the ways God shaped them through your prayers. What a heritage to pass down to them!

A nice bonus—this journal is completely guilt-free! You don't have to write in it every day. None of the journal pages are dated, so you'll never get the feeling you're behind. Just open it whenever you feel the need, and enjoy your time with God.

But it's also guilt-free in a better way. Anytime you face a shortcoming as you read and write your way through these pages, know that God isn't pointing the finger at you or your children. Instead, he delights when you recognize an area in which you need to improve. He's waiting with a smile and open arms. Run to him. He'll put his arm around you and walk with you. Lean on him, and feel his love.

Asking God to Shape Me into a Worthy Parent

Supply Wisdom as I Discipline My Children

Why It Is Important

Solomon, the smartest man who ever lived, wrote, "If you refuse to discipline your children, it proves you don't love them; if you love your children, you will be prompt to discipline them" (Prov. 13:24). Why? Because an undisciplined child grows into an adult who has trouble submitting to God's authority, a person who hurts himself as well as others.

It's not uncommon for very nice people to have trouble controlling the behavior of their offspring. Poor parenting begins early—maybe when kids won't stay in seatbelts and parents "just can't" make them buckle up. Next, parents look the other way when their toddler snatches a toy from a smaller child. Later, rather than insisting that their son complete his homework, parents complain that his teachers were unfair to assign it.

It's easy to let bad behavior slide; enforcing good behavior is hard work. Parents fear they might upset their children or even lose their love if they're too harsh. They don't realize that every time they let children manipulate them and win their own way, they're fostering the development of weak character.

Loving parents do everything in their power to shape their children into people of strong character. They discipline because they love their children too much not to. The best advice on discipline I ever got was in my first year of teaching:

"You can't care what the children think of you," an older sixth-grade teacher told me. "You have to do what's best for them." I offer that wise woman's words to every parent.

Why It Matters To You and Me

I was born with less common sense than the average person. When I follow the path that seems right to me, I usually mess up—badly. If God hadn't offered so much parenting advice in his Word, I would have failed miserably at the job. Fortunately, I spent a lot of time searching the Bible as my children were growing up. And every time I recognized my ineptitude and asked for wisdom, God gave it to me without a word of reprimand. Every ounce of wisdom I used in disciplining my children came from him. Okay—and from reading Dr. Dobson.

I made a lot of mistakes rearing my children, but I did a couple of things right. I sought the Scriptures for direction and prayed non-stop. I had no choice. I knew I lacked the ability to raise godly children without the Lord's constant help.

It doesn't matter how young or old your children are or how badly things seem to be going in your family right now—it's never too late to pray. So ask God for wisdom. He'll answer. You'll be shocked by the brilliant ideas that suddenly come to you and by the wise words that flow from your mouth.

Scripture Prayers You Can Pray for Your Children

- Lord, help me discipline _____ while there's hope. If I don't, I'll ruin his [her] life (see Prov. 19:18).

- Heavenly Father, don't let me fail to correct _____. He [She] won't die if I spank him [her]. Physical discipline may well save him [her] from death (see Prov. 23:13).

- Lord, I know that if I teach _____ to choose the right path, when he [she] is older he [she] will remain upon it (see Prov. 22:6).

- Help _____ listen and be wise. Keep his [her] heart on the right course (see Prov. 23:19).

- Heavenly Father, _____ is cause for joy. What a pleasure it is to have a wise child. Help him [her] give me joy! (see Prov. 23:24).

- Teach _____ to listen to the words of the wise, to apply his [her] heart to my instruction. For it's good to keep your sayings deep within, always ready on his [her] lips. Help me teach my child today so he [she] will trust in you (see Prov. 22:17–19).

Sharing My Thoughts with the Lord in Prayer

How this applies to my family and me

_____
_____
_____
_____
_____
_____
_____
_____
_____
_____

My specific prayer for:

_____
_____
_____
_____
_____
_____
_____
_____

Insights received as I prayed

_____
_____
_____
_____
_____

What I believe God will do

_____
_____
_____
_____
_____

Watching for answers:

Date and answer

_____
_____
_____
_____

Date and answer

_____
_____
_____
_____
_____

Date and answer

_____
_____
_____
_____

Help Me to Teach My Children about God

Why It Is Important

My friend Ron tells about waking in the middle of the night dripping with sweat, a nightmare still playing vividly in his mind. In this dream his oldest son, surrounded by ne'er-do-wells, leaned against a streetlight smoking, behaving like a bad guy from a cheap gangster movie.

Shaken, Ron crawled out of bed and dropped to his knees. "Why would I dream that, Lord?" he prayed. "My son is a wonderful boy. He's nothing like that kid in my dream."

The Lord spoke clearly to Ron's thoughts: "Yes, but if you fail to teach him about me and pray for him, that's what he could become." Ron heeded the warning and faithfully taught his son about the Lord. He also prayed for him daily. Today his son is an exemplary man.

Why It Matters To You and Me

A May 2003 Barna report states that close to nine out of ten parents with children under the age of thirteen accept primary responsibility for instilling religious beliefs in their children. The majority of those parents attend church at least once a month and take their children along when they go, but they spend no time during the week discussing religious matters with their children. As a result, most children get no more than one or two hours of religious instruction a week (Barna Research Online, "Parents Accept Responsibility for Their Child's Spiritual Development but Struggle with Effectiveness," www.barna.org, May 6, 2003). That's far less time than they spend attending school, participating in sporting activities, or watching television. And it falls far short of God's command that parents integrate teachings about him into every activity (see Deut. 6:6, 7).

Given the above information, does it surprise you that of the fifty-one million children under the age of eighteen who live in the United States, more than forty million do not know Jesus Christ as their Savior (Barna Research Online, "Parents Accept Responsibility. . . .)? God holds you ultimately responsible to instruct your children about him. Don't let that scare you—it's an honor.

- Study the Book of Proverbs in the Old Testament. Written by the smartest man who ever lived, it's brimming with parenting tips. If you follow his advice, your kids will understand how to live righteous lives that please the Lord.

- Share a verse or two from Proverbs with your children each day. Require them to memorize one per week.

- As you drive to and from sports practice and when you tuck the kids into bed, teach them the things you're learning about the Lord.

- Pray with your children when any problem arises.

Teaching your children about God should be exciting. It's amazing to watch them accept him and change. Since God wants to function as your support team, ask him to. Ask him for heart knowledge as well as head knowledge. Tell him you reject any dry form of religion and choose to burn with the fire of his presence. He won't let you down. And your children will internalize your example. God will shape you and your children into vibrant Christians.

Scripture Prayers You Can Pray for Your Children

- O God, help me commit myself wholeheartedly to the commands you have given. Help me repeat them again and again to _____. Help me talk about them when we're at home and when we're away on a journey, when we're lying down and when we're getting up again (see Deut. 6:6, 7).

- Help me warn and teach _____ with all the wisdom you have given me. For I want to present him [her] to you, perfect in his [her] relationship to you. Help me work very hard at this, as I depend on your mighty power that works within me (see Col. 1:28, 29).

- Heavenly Father, _____ is but a foreigner here on earth. He [She] needs the guidance of your commands. Don't hide them from him [her]! Continually overwhelm him [her] with a desire for your laws (see Ps. 119:19, 20).

- Call _____ to search for the Lord my God with his [her] whole heart and soul. I know he [she] will find him (see Deut. 4:29).

- Help _____ follow my advice and always treasure your commands. Help him [her] obey them and live. Make him [her] guard my teachings as his [her] most precious possession. Guide him [her] to write them deep within his [her] heart (see Prov. 7:1–3).

- Teach my son [daughter] to pay attention to my wisdom. Make him [her] listen carefully to my wise counsel. Then he [she] will learn to be discreet and will store up knowledge (see Prov. 5:1, 2).

Sharing My Thoughts with the Lord in Prayer

How this applies to my family and me

_____
_____
_____
_____
_____
_____
_____
_____
_____
_____

My specific prayer for:

_____
_____
_____
_____
_____
_____
_____
_____

Insights received as I prayed

_____
_____
_____
_____
_____
_____

What I believe God will do

_____
_____
_____
_____
_____
_____

Watching for answers:

Date and answer

_____
_____
_____
_____
_____

Date and answer

_____
_____
_____
_____

Date and answer

_____
_____
_____
_____
_____

Keep Me from Hindering God's Work in Them

Why It Is Important

I'll never forget the day I saw Matt's face flash across the screen of the television court show—at least it looked like Matt. Stunned by that face and the words I heard, I stopped dusting and sank onto the couch, my eyes glued to the screen. Maybe, hopefully, the defendant on the show only looked like Matt. After all, the judge kept calling him by a different name, and it had been two years since I taught him in Christian school. Kids change a lot between junior high and high school. The face looked like Matt's, and the voice sounded like Matt's, but I could be wrong, couldn't I?

The boy's mother had brought him to television court in an effort to quash his rebellious behavior. "He's out of control—he smokes and drinks," she told the judge. "I can't do anything with Matt." She didn't seem to notice she had used his real name, but her slip confirmed my suspicions. The boy on the screen was my former student. "He uses drugs and says he wants to kill someone."

"Is that true?" The same shock I felt flickered across the judge's face.

"Yes," he replied, lifting his chin and grinning the way I had seen him do when he got caught doing something wrong at school. "I will kill someone," he said, his eyes narrowing, "and I hope it's a Christian. I hate Christians." A cold lump of grief formed in the pit of my stomach.

"Young man, you are headed straight to prison," the judge said.

Matt shrugged. I cried through the rest of show. I loved Matt. He often stayed to talk to me after class. I had seen a sweetness in him, even though he informed me once that he wanted nothing to do with the Lord. How did he end up as the boy I was watching on television?

Then I remembered his mother's reactions whenever Matt got into trouble at school. When teachers disciplined him, she would storm into the classroom, insisting that they were treating him unfairly. As a result, Matt was never forced to confront his own failings.

Why It Matters To You and Me

What a shame that Matt's mother refused to face the truth about her son until things had gone so far! Oswald Chambers says, "When you see a person . . . in the middle of a difficult and painful struggle, don't try to prevent it, but pray that his difficulty will grow ten times stronger, until no power on earth or in hell could hold him away from Jesus Christ."

My pastor, Ron Mehl, said it in a cuter way: "I give God permission to slap my boys around any time they get off track and need his discipline."

It's hard to do as those two wise men suggest. Every time my children mess up, I want to hurry to their aid. The problem is, God uses difficult circumstances to teach and develop godly character. If I get in his way, they may never become people he can use.

So I pray often for God give me wisdom to know when I should offer advice, when I should help, and when I should step back and let him teach my children through natural consequences. Practicing tough love may be difficult, but it's necessary for parents who want godly children.

Scripture Prayers You Can Pray for Your Children

- Help _____ not to ignore your discipline and not to be discouraged when you correct her [him]. For you discipline those you love, and you punish those you accept as your children (see Heb. 12:7).

- Remind _____ that no discipline is enjoyable while it is happening—it is painful! But afterward there will be a quiet harvest of right living for those who are trained this way (see Heb. 12:11).

- Heavenly Father, don't let _____ ignore your discipline. Keep her [him] from becoming discouraged when you correct her [him]. For you correct those you love, just as a father corrects a child in whom he delights (see Prov. 3:11).

- Help my children to be happy when you discipline them, Lord, and when you teach them from your law (see Ps. 94:12).

- Lord, I know when you judge and discipline _____ he [she] will not be condemned with the world (see 1 Cor. 11:32). Thank you.

Sharing My Thoughts with the Lord in Prayer

How this applies to my family
and me

_____
_____
_____
_____
_____
_____
_____
_____
_____
_____

My specific prayer for:

_____
_____
_____
_____
_____
_____
_____
_____

Insights received as I prayed

_____
_____
_____
_____
_____

What I believe God will do

_____
_____
_____
_____
_____
_____

Watching for answers:

Date and answer

_____
_____
_____
_____

Date and answer

_____
_____
_____
_____
_____

Date and answer

_____
_____
_____
_____

Help Me Model
Encouraging Words

Why It Is Important

Words matter. God spoke, and the universe sprang into being. The apostle John called Jesus "the Word"—"In the beginning the Word already existed. He was with God, and he was God" (John 1:1). The Bible, God's living Word for us, powerfully changes lives. We use words to form prayers that move the hand of God.

But not all words are good. Satan twists words and distorts their meaning. He lies. He accuses. Words inspired by Satan damage people and relationships.

Jesus said we couldn't keep from showing who we are when we speak, no matter how we try to hide it. "For whatever is in your heart determines what you say. A good person produces good words from a good heart, and an evil person produces evil words from an evil heart" (Matt. 12:34, 35).

I'll admit to being an imperfect human whose words don't always encourage and uplift the way I would like them to. Fortunately, as I yield myself to Jesus and allow him to draw my heart to him, the words coming from my mouth get sweeter and wiser. I'm so grateful.

Why It Matters To You and Me

Your words powerfully affect your children.

- Your words can stir up anger or soothe it. "A gentle answer turns away wrath, but harsh words stir up anger" (Prov. 15:1).

- Your words can refresh and teach. "A person's words can be life-giving water; words of true wisdom are as refreshing as a bubbling brook" (Prov. 18:4).

- Your words can nourish their souls and heal their bodies. "Kind words are like honey—sweet to the soul and healthy for the body" (Prov. 16:24).

- Your advice is precious to your children. "Timely advice is as lovely as golden apples in a silver basket (Prov. 25:11).

- Your timely rebuke will impart wisdom. "It is better to be criticized by a wise person than to be praised by a fool!" (Eccles. 7:5).

- Your words can speak death or life to your children. "The words of the wicked are like a murderous ambush, but the words of the godly save lives" (Prov. 12:6).

If you find yourself speaking words that wound, ask God to cleanse and purify your heart so healing words will flow from you. Recognize that hurtful, blaming words come from Satan. Allow the Holy Spirit to take control of your tongue.

If it is already your habit to offer words that bless and encourage, praise the Lord! Keep it up! Kind words are contagious. Your children are picking up that skill without even realizing it. If you haven't seen it in them yet, you will. The ripple effect has already begun. First your words will influence your children; then their good words will impact more people than you could ever imagine.

Pray for the Lord to work in your children's hearts so the words they speak will bless and encourage many.

Scripture Prayers You Can Pray for Your Children

- O God, there is more hope for a fool than for someone who speaks without thinking. So help _____ measure her [his] words before she [he] speaks (see Prov. 29:20).

- When worry weighs _____ down, show me how to cheer her [him] up with encouraging words (see Prov. 12:25).

- Help _____ avoid all perverse talk and stay away from corrupt speech (see Prov. 4:24).

- Enable _____ to control his [her] tongue. If he [she] learns to do that, he [she] will also be able to control himself [herself] in every other way (see James 3:2).

- Help _____ listen to the words of the wise and apply his [her] heart to your instruction. For it is good for him [her] to keep wise words deep within himself [herself], always ready on his [her] lips (see Prov. 22:17–18).

Sharing My Thoughts with the Lord in Prayer

How this applies to my Family and me

_____
_____
_____
_____
_____
_____
_____
_____
_____
_____

My specific prayer for:

_____
_____
_____
_____
_____
_____
_____
_____

Insights received as I prayed

_____
_____
_____
_____
_____
_____

What I believe God will do

_____
_____
_____
_____
_____
_____
_____

Watching for answers:

Date and answer

_____
_____
_____
_____
_____

Date and answer

_____
_____
_____
_____
_____

Date and answer

_____
_____
_____
_____
_____

Teach Me to Look to You
When Problems Seem
Insurmountable

Why It Is Important

I can't remember the number of times I've begged God for help with my children when I faced a seemingly impossible situation. I asked him to protect the life of my daughter while I carried her through a difficult pregnancy. As a result, my placenta did not separate prematurely as doctors expected. That seemed a miracle to me. I begged for mercy and wisdom to raise my son wisely after three-year-old Ty caught and killed one of our chickens with his bare hands. God formed Ty into a godly man instead of the serial killer I feared he would become. After much prayer, my shyest child became confident and charming. That may not sound like much to you, but it felt miraculous to me.

Of all the impossible situations I faced, I'm most grateful for the time God answered when I threw myself spread eagle across the washing machine, sobbing and telling Jesus I couldn't stand the constant bickering between my three elementary-age children anymore. They rarely fought after that. If you don't know that was a miracle, you're the parent of an only child!

Someday you'll face one of those impossible situations with your children. I can guarantee it. If your preemie's lungs don't require miraculous healing, your elementary school child may struggle with a learning disability or spend months in a coma after an accident. Your middle schooler's open rebellion will help you understand that only God's grace can save him or her from destruction.

Even after your children are successfully grown and out of the house, other problems can surface: job loss, financial problems, adultery, pornography, depression, divorce, infertility, cancer, loss through flood or tornado—the list is endless. In *The Road Less Traveled,* M. Scott Peck tells us life is difficult, but Jesus said it first. "Here on earth you will have many trials and sorrows" (John 16:33)—count on it.

Why It Matters To You and Me

God can rescue your children from impossible difficulties, but he usually does it in response to prayer. And the one person responsible to pray for your children is . . . you.

Think about it. How often do you pray for someone else's children? Not often, right? That's approximately how much prayer your kids will get from anyone besides you. If you don't pray for them, no one will. That's a scary thought, isn't it?

The good news is that God can do anything, and he'll answer your prayers. You don't have to be a pastor or an apostle to have God solve impossible situations for you. The book of James in the New Testament tells us that Elijah was a man just like us. Yet when he prayed, God did something impossible— he held back the rain for three years. When Elijah prayed again, God sent another impossible answer. Black clouds crowded the sky, Elijah's robe whipped in the wind, and God poured torrents of water from the heavens.

There was a condition to it, though. Elijah's prayer lined up with God's will, and he didn't just sit on the couch with folded hands and mumble a quiet request. He climbed to the top of a mountain where he fell to the ground, praying fervently. Desperate for a miracle, he begged God for rain. I can almost hear his tears and shouts alternating with deep groans.

The verse in James that describes how Elijah prayed is awkward when translated literally from the Greek, but it means that Elijah prayed earnestly with lots of energy. That's the kind of prayer that calls forth God's miracles. If you want help for your children when things seem unsolvable, don't be shy and pray halfheartedly—pray with your whole being. Let God know how desperately you need him.

Then keep asking until he answers—no matter how long it takes. Elijah prayed for hours on the day God sent the rainstorm. You may have to pray longer, but it doesn't matter. Just keep praying. God will always send the help you need, even when the situation seems impossible.

Scripture Prayers You Can Pray for Your Children

- Jesus, teach _____ that though humanly speaking things may be impossible, with God everything is possible (see Matt. 19:26).

- Show _____ that anything is possible if a person believes (see Mark 9:23).

- Heavenly Father, please give _____ your Holy Spirit. Work miracles among us because we believe the message we heard about Christ (see Gal. 3:5).

- Jesus, teach _____ that what is impossible from a human perspective is possible with you (see Luke 18:27).

- God, show _____ that all human help is useless. With your help he [she] will do mighty things, for you will trample down his [her] foes (see Ps. 108:12, 13).

Sharing My Thoughts with the Lord in Prayer

How this applies to my family and me

_____
_____
_____
_____
_____
_____
_____
_____
_____

My specific prayer for:

_____
_____
_____
_____
_____
_____
_____

Insights received as I prayed

_____
_____
_____
_____
_____

What I believe God will do

_____
_____
_____
_____
_____

Watching for answers:

Date and answer

_____
_____
_____
_____

Date and answer

_____
_____
_____
_____

Date and answer

_____
_____
_____
_____

Requesting Protection and Health for My Child

Spread an Umbrella of Protection over My Children

Why It Is Important

Back when I was growing up in Ohio, it would have seemed silly to write a chapter on praying for protection. Thirty years ago, most parts of our country seemed fairly safe, and parents didn't have to worry so much about the security of their children. We didn't lock our doors. I don't remember any kidnappings, but I do remember feeling safe. One time my mother left me in charge of my younger siblings for three days while she and my father left on a trip. I was eleven and not one bit scared.

As a teenager I loved taking long walks after dark, gazing up at the stars. Nothing bad ever happened. The closest our family ever came to tragedy centered around the time my sister accidentally climbed into a stranger's car. She was looking out the living room window, waiting for a friend to pick her up, when a dark green sedan stopped in front of our house. It looked like the right car. She rushed out, opened the back door, crawled in, and slammed the door behind her. The car didn't move. The people in the front seat snickered. She fled back into the house, red-faced. I doubt she even apologized.

It's different today. Stories about young girls who innocently enter strangers' cars don't always end happily. All it takes to send shivers down any parent's spine is to mention a few names: Elizabeth Smart. Polly Klass. Ted Bundy. The world is not a safe place. Our children need protection.

Why It Matters To You and Me

While "stranger danger" lurks at the back of most parents' minds, all sorts of hazards abound in our world. To name a few: auto accidents, fatal diseases, head injuries, broken bones. . . . If you and I sat and brainstormed everything that could go wrong to hurt our children, we would be talking for hours. Even then, we couldn't cover every possibility. I recently saw a story on the news about a plane crashing into an apartment building and killing four people. How could parents predict something like that? Plus—emotional health is at least as important as physical health. "Sticks and stones may break my bones, but words can never hurt me" is a lie. Everyone knows that.

You would do anything to protect your children from those frightening things. So would I. There's a lot we can do. We should warn our sons against dashing out in front of moving cars, we should teach our daughters to wash their hands and avoid many illnesses, but there's nothing we can do to avoid all peril.

That's why I lift "umbrella prayers" of protection over my children. Though I can't anticipate and prevent all problems, God foresees every threat. He has the power to take care of my children, and he wants to. So every morning I ask him to dispatch mighty angels to spread wings over them like a giant umbrella. I ask him not to let anything Satan aims at my kids penetrate that umbrella. Then I sigh and give him permission to do whatever he needs to do. If he chooses to allow some difficulties, I'll accept that.

You can do it too. Lift an umbrella of prayer over your children to shield them from harm today. Do it every single day of their lives. Ask God to protect their bodies, minds, and spirits. God will protect them. He promised. Your children won't avoid every pitfall, but you can be certain God will use every problem to shape them into strong, godly people.

Thank him for his protection.

Scripture Prayers You Can Pray for Your Children

- O Lord, be a shield around _____. Let him [her] lie down and sleep and then wake up in safety, for you are watching over him [her]. Keep him [her] from being afraid—even if ten thousand enemies surround him [her] on every side (see Ps. 3:3, 5–6).

- Order your angels to protect _____ wherever she [he] goes (see Ps. 91:11).

- Keep _____ living in the shelter of you, the Most High. Let her [him] find rest in the shadow of you, the Almighty. You alone are her [his] refuge. You are her [his] God. Help her [him] trust in you (see Ps. 91:1–2).

- Lord, you said you will rescue those who love you. You will protect those who trust in your name. When they call on you, you will answer. So be with _____ in trouble. Rescue him [her] and honor him [her]. Satisfy him [her] with a long life, and give him [her] your salvation (see Ps. 91:14–16).

- Jesus, help _____ be strong with the Lord's mighty power. Teach her [him] to put on all of God's armor so that she [he] will be able to stand firm against all strategies and tricks of the devil. For she [he] is fighting not against people made of flesh and blood but against evil rulers and authorities of the unseen world, against those mighty powers of darkness who rule this world, and against wicked spirits in the heavenly realms. Teach her [him] to use every piece of God's armor to resist the enemy in the time of evil, so that after the battle she [he] will be standing firm (see Eph. 6:10–13).

Sharing My Thoughts with the Lord in Prayer

How this applies to my family and me

_____
_____
_____
_____
_____
_____
_____
_____
_____
_____

My specific prayer for:

_____
_____
_____
_____
_____
_____
_____

Insights received as I prayed

_____
_____
_____
_____

What I believe God will do

_____
_____
_____
_____
_____
_____
_____

Watching for answers:

Date and answer

_____
_____
_____
_____

Date and answer

_____
_____
_____
_____
_____

Date and answer

_____
_____
_____
_____

Protect Them from Bullying

Why It Is Important

To this day my son has no idea why the boy sporting spiked red hair and a studded leather jacket jostled him as they passed through the locker room door. The kid was an eighth-grader; Ty was a sixth-grader. Ty didn't even know him, so he assumed it was an accidental collision, just one of those things that happens. He mumbled, "Sorry," and continued into the locker room to change for class.

Setting his books down onto a bench, he reached for the locker door. Wham! Something from behind slammed his head into the metal locker. Stunned, Ty turned to face his attacker. The redheaded boy balled his fist and slugged Ty again. And again. Ty stumbled away, glancing around for help. No teacher was on duty. Several of his classmates stared, but none offered assistance. Ty would have to defend himself.

The boy charged again, but this time Ty was ready. He had never fought before, but he had played football since the fourth grade. Hunkering into position, he waited. When the boy rushed him, Ty banged into the kid's mid-section with his head. The boy fell backward, then straightened and came at Ty again. Before the boy could make contact, my son butted him in the stomach for the second time. It didn't take too many thumps before Ty's attacker fled the scene.

After school, when Ty showed me his injuries, I was furious with the bully as well as the school who failed to protect my son. Yet at the same time, I felt so proud Ty had the self-control to fight only in self-defense as we had taught him. My son may have been the victim of bullying, but I knew he would never stoop to being a bully himself.

Years later I recognize how God used that incident to shape Ty into a more sensitive young man. He never forgot the kids who watched the locker-room attack and did nothing to help. He determined that he would always come to the aid of anyone in trouble. Though he has never had to fight again, he has kept that promise. If you're ever in danger, you might want to call Ty.

Why It Matters To You and Me

Most children are bullied at one time or another. If they aren't physically threatened, giggling cliques ridicule them. Not all youngsters react to this treatment in a positive way. Many victims seethe with resentment and nurse thoughts of revenge. The most damaged victims-turned-bullies are responsible for school shootings. Kids who respond slightly better physically and verbally abuse spouses when grown.

You can help your children react correctly when mistreated. Teach them to forgive by turning bitterness and anger over to God. Pray with them so they'll learn to take all problems to the Lord. Pray for them not to fear but rather to trust God for protection. Ask the Lord to protect them from anyone who would victimize them. Ask him to fill them with a confidence that demands others treat them with respect. But most important, ask God to make your children compassionate and loving, people who would never bully anyone.

Scripture Prayers You Can Pray for Your Children

- Teach _____ never to pay back evil for evil to anyone. Help him [her] do things in such a way that everyone can see that he [she] is honorable. Enable him [her] to live in peace with everyone as much as is possible. Help him [her] never to avenge himself [herself] but to leave it to you. For it is written, "I will take vengeance; I will repay those who deserve it" (see Rom. 12:17–19).

- Help _____ to love her [his] neighbor so she [he] will fulfill all the requirements of your law. For the commandments are all summed up in this one commandment: "Love your neighbor as yourself." Love does no wrong to anyone, so love satisfies all of your requirements (see Rom. 13:8–10).

- Help _____ and _____ show love among themselves, because if they are always biting and devouring one another, they could destroy one another (see Gal. 5:15).

- Teach_____ to stand up for the poor and helpless and see that they get justice (see Prov. 31:9).

- Help _____ follow your example in everything she [he] does, because she [he] is your dear child. Let her [him] live a life filled with love for others, following the example of your Son, who loved her [him] and gave himself as a sacrifice to take away her [his] sins (see Eph. 5:1, 2).

Sharing My Thoughts with the Lord in Prayer

How this applies to my family and me

_____
_____
_____
_____
_____
_____
_____
_____
_____
_____
_____

My specific prayer for:

_____
_____
_____
_____
_____
_____
_____

Insights received as I prayed

_____
_____
_____
_____
_____

What I believe God will do

_____
_____
_____
_____
_____
_____
_____

Watching for answers:

Date and answer

_____
_____
_____
_____
_____

Date and answer

_____
_____
_____
_____
_____

Date and answer

_____
_____
_____
_____
_____

Protect Them from Generational Sins

Why It Is Important

I hate to tell you this, but I crack stupid jokes, puns mostly. I don't do it deliberately. They just pop into my mind unbidden, and I can't keep from blurting them out. When my children hear them, they roll their eyes or groan and shake their heads.

I blame my father, the pun king. Either his love of puns pounced on me like a contagious disease, or there's something strange about the way brains are wired in our family. And I've passed the problem along to my own three children. Occasionally at first, but now quite often, one of them will crack a joke, then slap palm to forehead and cry out, "Oh, no—I made a Mom joke!"

My youngest son's worst nightmare came true recently when he and I responded in unison, and with identical jokes, to a statement my husband made. As soon as the words exited our mouths, my son began moaning in mock despair. I chuckled.

I would love to tell you that cracking silly jokes is the most serious problem my children inherited from me. It isn't. Several specific sins, sometimes called generational sins, slipped from my grandparents to my parents to me and then to my children in much the same way making puns trickled down my family line.

A flaw that propels my children to tell dumb jokes is amusing. Generational sins are not. They damage relationships and ruin bright futures. They require much prayer.

Why It Matters To You and Me

I would be surprised to find a family without generational sins. All families have them, including yours. Alcoholism, lying, and sexual deviancy are easy to spot. "Nicer" sins, such as pride, laziness, and hypocrisy, not only are more difficult to detect but are also often viewed as almost harmless. They aren't. Their tendrils snake past our deliberate acts and reach into our unconscious, gripping our very souls with an invisible iron fist.

"I don't understand myself at all," Paul says. "I really want to do what is right, but I don't do it. Instead, I do the very thing I hate" (see Rom. 7:15). He is speaking of all sin, but I think his words especially fit generational sins. "I can't help myself, because it is sin inside me that makes me do these evil things. Oh, what a miserable person I am! Who will free me from this life that is dominated by sin?" (see Rom. 7:24).

God will free you and your children if you go to him in prayer. Wait on him, pleading with him to reveal the generational sins in your family line. Then stay aware and on the lookout for them. Ask Jesus to make you willing to recognize and confess every generational sin. Have your children memorize verses that will help them stand against those sins.

Then, since you are powerless against sin without his help, pray again. Pray fervently. Lift the sins to him one by one. Repent. Request forgiveness for your forefathers and yourself. Beg him to cleanse you of those sins and heal you so the damage will stop with you and not creep into your children's lives.

If your children have grown past the toddler years, chances are that generational sins already have a hold on them. Don't be discouraged. Instead, ask the Lord to free them. Call on the name of Jesus and his power to cancel all Satan's authority over you and your children. Ask him to cleanse your family line. This may require much time in fervent prayer, but God can do it, and he will do it.

Scripture Prayers You Can Pray for Your Children

- Just as the Israelites separated themselves and confessed their own sins and the sins of their ancestors, I confess my sins, _____'s sins, and the sins of my ancestors (see Neh. 9:2).

- Lord, your Word says that you punish children of the parents who hate you to the third and fourth generations. First cleanse me, and then make _____ into a person who loves you and obeys your commands so you can lavish your love on him [her] and also on my future grandchildren (see Exod. 20:5, 6).

- Have mercy on me, O God. Blot out the stain of my sins. Wash me clean from my guilt. Purify _____ from sin, and he [she] will be clean; wash him [her], and he [she] will be whiter than snow (see Ps. 51:1–2, 7).

- Lord, help _____ test and examine her [his] ways. Let her [him] turn in repentance to you. Let her [him] lift up her [his] heart and hands to God in heaven (see Lam. 3:40–41).

- How can _____ know all the sins lurking in his [her] heart? Cleanse him [her] from these hidden faults. Keep him [her] from deliberate sins! Don't let them control him [her]. Then he [she] will be free of guilt and innocent of great sin (see Ps. 19:12–13).

Sharing My Thoughts with the Lord in Prayer

How this applies to my family
and me

_____
_____
_____
_____
_____
_____
_____
_____
_____
_____
_____

My specific prayer for:

_____
_____
_____
_____
_____
_____
_____

Insights received as I prayed

_____
_____
_____
_____
_____

What I believe God will do

_____
_____
_____
_____
_____
_____

Watching for answers:

Date and answer

_____
_____
_____
_____

Date and answer

_____
_____
_____

Date and answer

_____
_____
_____

Deliver Them from False Guilt

Why It Is Important

Ruth felt compelled to tell the female counselor about her past. Head bowed, tears streaming down her face, she whispered the shame that had caused her anguish for thirty years. When she finally paused to compose herself, the counselor's matter-of-fact tone broke through her despair. "Has God already forgiven those sins?"

Ruth looked up, surprised. "Yes, I asked Jesus to forgive me years ago." She was a Christian. She knew the Bible verses that promised God's forgiveness, but she still felt ashamed.

"Well then," said the counselor. "I want you to remember that the purpose of true guilt is to send us to the Father for forgiveness. Once we've done that, any residual guilt is not coming from God but from Satan, the Accuser. When those perverse sins come to mind, here's what I want you to do."

The woman sat up straight and squared her shoulders. "Repeat Romans 8:1: 'There is no condemnation for those who belong to Christ Jesus' and refuse to feel shame. Be proud you know a God powerful enough to change you from that perverted person into the new creation you are today. Be grateful because the memory of who you were reminds you to praise your Savior."

The counselor tipped up her chin and gazed heavenward, her face glowing. "Then thank God for making you clean and giving you this unique opportunity praise to your Father. Keep praising him until thoughts of his goodness and mercy fill your mind and Satan, the Accuser, is forced to slink away."

Over the next few weeks, Ruth practiced the counselor's advice, thanking and praising God each time she remembered her former sins. Gradually her false guilt disappeared, and she realized she had suffered needlessly for thirty years.

Why It Matters To You and Me

James says that all good and perfect gifts come from God. Bad feelings from true guilt are so horrible that they may not seem like a good gift to us, but they are. Before we were saved, God sent guilt feelings so that grief and remorse over wrong thoughts and actions would drive us to repentance. Once we ask for forgiveness, all guilt feelings should disappear.

So why do we still feel guilty after we've been forgiven, even though God intended guilt feelings simply as a temporary measure to open our eyes to truth and soften our hearts?

For every good gift of God, Satan offers an imitation. When we repent and God lifts our true guilt, the Accuser does his best to load false guilt onto our shoulders. The false guilt feels worse than the true guilt because, unlike the guilt God removes, false guilt stays with us. We get relief only when we recognize false guilt as coming from our enemy and reject it.

Pray for your children to learn how to accept God's forgiveness and avoid the pain of false guilt.

Scripture Prayers You Can Pray for Your Children

- Show _____ that all have sinned and fallen short of your glorious standard. Yet now you in your gracious kindness declare _____ not guilty. You have done this through Jesus Christ, who has freed us by taking away our sins (see Rom. 3:23, 24).

- Convince _____ that there is no condemnation for those who belong to Christ Jesus, who do not walk according to the flesh but according to the Spirit. For the power of the life-giving Spirit has freed _____ from the power of sin that leads to death (see Rom. 8:1, 2).

- Reveal to _____ that it is Satan who accuses Christians day and night (see Rev. 12:10).

- Teach _____ that it is not you who constantly accuses (see Ps. 103:9).

- Remind _____ that you have removed our rebellious acts as far away from us as the east is from the west (see Ps. 103:12).

Sharing My Thoughts with the Lord in Prayer

How this applies to my family
and me

_____
_____
_____
_____
_____
_____
_____
_____
_____
_____
_____

My specific prayer for:

_____
_____
_____
_____
_____
_____
_____
_____
_____

Insights received as I prayed

_____
_____
_____
_____
_____

What I believe God will do

_____
_____
_____
_____
_____
_____

Watching for answers:

Date and answer

_____
_____
_____
_____
_____

Date and answer

_____
_____
_____
_____
_____
_____

Date and answer

_____
_____
_____
_____

Praying for Healthy Emotions

Keep Them From Comparing
Themselves to Others

Why It Is Important

I learned about numbers when my parents taught me to count from one to one hundred, long before I ever stepped foot in first grade. There was something comforting about the structure numbers added to my life. Numbers told me that I had two feet and ten fingers, but my Grandpa Perry was missing one thumb and one finger. They told me my little sister was three years younger than I. When I counted out the contents of my piggy bank onto my upper bunk, numbers showed me that I had to save exactly five more pennies to buy a jar of marshmallow creme.

I could trust numbers—or at least I thought I could. All that changed when my son, Ty, shattered my confidence by informing me that in higher mathematics there are other kinds of numbers. I only knew about one kind—real numbers that march along in order, numbers that leave no doubt of their value.

Ty told me complex numbers are different. While they do have a real part, they have an imaginary side too. Even if you know what all the parts are—say the real part is two and the imaginary part is negative three i—complex numbers can't be put in order. Complex numbers can't be compared. They're just different. Yet even though there's no way to figure out if one number is worth more than another, they each have value.

Why It Matters To You and Me

Ty told me he believes that without a divine perspective, we evaluate people the way we use real numbers—some people are obviously better looking, smarter, or more athletic. However, God wants us to value people by his system, which we could look at as complex numbers. We see physical appearance and talents; but there are parts of every person we can't see and evaluate. We need to realize each individual is unique and valuable to God. He doesn't compare us.

Comparison doesn't work. A dinner plate can't be compared to a drinking glass. A dog can't be compared to a horse. One is not better than the other—they're just different. At the end of the twenty-first chapter of John, when Peter tried to compare himself to John, Jesus wouldn't let him. He indicated that Peter should simply follow him without worrying about the other disciple.

Yet we still strive to compare ourselves, which makes us feel either inadequate or proud. Comparing ourselves causes dissatisfaction, because there will always be someone else prettier, smarter, richer, more creative, wittier, or more athletic than we are. Even those rare people who find themselves at the top won't stay there forever. Is Lillian Gish still one of the most beautiful actresses on the big screen? Is Bill Clinton the most powerful politician in the United States today? Superficial achievements that seem so important to us don't matter to God. He loves and values us simply because we belong to him.

Pray that your children will never compare themselves to others. Pray for them to be satisfied, striving simply to become the person God created them to be.

Scripture Prayers You Can Pray for Your Children

- Please keep _____ and _____ from comparing themselves with each other and measuring themselves by themselves. What foolishness! (see 2 Cor. 10:12).

- Lord, help _____ do what she [he] should, for then she [he] will enjoy the personal satisfaction of having done her [his] work well, and she [he] won't need to compare herself [himself] to anyone else. For we are each responsible for our own conduct (see Gal. 6:4).

- Teach _____ that you have given each of us the ability to do certain things well (see Rom. 12:6).

- Help _____ be honest in his [her] estimate of himself [herself], measuring his [her] value by how much faith you have given him [her] (see Rom. 12:3).

- Teach _____ that all of us together are Christ's body, and each one of us is a separate and necessary part of it (see 1 Cor. 12:27).

- Make it _____'s purpose to please you and not people. You are the one who examines the motives of our hearts (see 1 Thess. 2:4).

Sharing My Thoughts with the Lord in Prayer

How this applies to my family and me

_____
_____
_____
_____
_____
_____
_____
_____
_____
_____

My specific prayer for:

_____
_____
_____
_____
_____
_____
_____
_____

Insights received as I prayed

_____
_____
_____
_____
_____

What I believe God will do

_____
_____
_____
_____
_____
_____

Watching for answers:

Date and answer

_____
_____
_____
_____

Date and answer

_____
_____
_____
_____

Date and answer

_____
_____
_____
_____
_____

Please Grant
My Children Happiness

Why It Is Important

Three months before the birth of my first child, doctors used forceps to deliver a friend's baby. That little girl ended up paralyzed on one side, and the doctors had no idea if she would recover or not. It terrified me. I knew my own doctor often delivered using forceps. I began imagining the problems my child would face if he had to grow up paralyzed. Fear for him churned around in my brain. I got more and more upset.

Since I react to fear with aggression, a week later I marched hands-on-hips to my appointment with my obstetrician and informed him that he would not under any circumstances use forceps on my child's head. I would never do anything to cause my child's suffering, and I certainly refused to give my doctor permission to do so either. My child would have a happy, carefree life.

My doctor, a Christian gentleman, sat down on his padded-leather stool, arms crossed, head cocked to one side. He could not promise not to use forceps, he told me gently but firmly. He would do whatever he felt necessary to safely deliver my baby. More important, he said, everyone must deal with difficulties in life—even my child. I needed to learn I could not always protect him. It was impossible for me to guarantee my child's happiness. The best I could do was pray and trust God with him.

Though I hated the man's words, I recognized the wisdom in them.

Three months later, he did use forceps on my son before finally delivering him by Caesarian section. God protected Ty. The forceps didn't hurt him one bit. My friend's daughter recovered too. God took care of everything without help from me.

Why It Matters To You and Me

We all want happiness for our children. There's nothing wrong with that, of course. God wants it, too. The problem is that we live in a fallen world. We can't avoid trouble.

Plus, because we don't understand what true happiness is, we strive for the wrong things. Remember the Texas mother who hired a hit man to kill the teenage girl she feared might win her daughter's spot on the cheerleading squad? The mother did it to ensure her daughter's happiness, even though cheerleading could never bring true happiness.

True happiness comes only from the Lord, and we can choose to have it. The apostle Paul exhorts us to be full of joy in the Lord always—rejoicing all the time and in everything. It's the best way to ensure happiness. We choose joy when we concentrate on things that are pure and lovely and admirable. We choose contentment when we think about excellent things. It's a choice.

It's pointless to ask God to shield your children from all problems. He won't. Trials develop the godly character he desires. So ask him to give them joy in the midst of trouble. Pray for them to choose joy by learning to trust and rejoice in him no matter what happens. There's a bonus in it for them. The joy of the Lord will be their strength—despite the circumstances.

Scripture Prayers You Can Pray for Your Children

- Teach _____ that those who listen to instruction will prosper and those who trust you will be happy (see Prov. 16:20).

- Don't let _____ be dejected and sad, for the joy of the Lord is her [his] strength (see Neh. 8:10).

- Make _____ walk along the path of your commands, for that is where his [her] happiness is found (see Ps. 119:35).

- Give _____ happiness, O Lord, for her [his] life depends on you (see Ps. 86:4).

- Teach _____ to get along happily whether he [she] has much or little. Teach him [her] how to live on almost nothing or with everything. Teach him [her] the secret of living in every situation (see Phil. 4:11, 12).

Sharing My Thoughts with the Lord in Prayer

How this applies to my family and me

_____
_____
_____
_____
_____
_____
_____
_____
_____

My specific prayer for:

_____
_____
_____
_____
_____
_____
_____

Insights received as I prayed

_____
_____
_____
_____

What I believe God will do

_____
_____
_____
_____
_____

Watching for answers:

Date and answer

_____
_____
_____
_____

Date and answer

_____
_____
_____
_____

Date and answer

_____
_____
_____
_____

Give Them Good Attitudes

Why It Is Important

I remember Carolyn as an I-can-do-it-myself little girl with wild blonde curls and eyes the color of a summer sky. At age nine, she had a mind of her own, plucking her dad's tender young zucchini plants from the garden while pretending to weed. She hated vegetables and didn't care who knew it.

Ripping up those little plants took effort, however, because by then an incurable disease called Nieman Picks had begun to eat away at her muscles. The piano teacher noticed it first when Carolyn's nimble fingers became increasingly clumsy on the keys, even though she practiced diligently. By age sixteen her speech was slurred, and she aspirated food or water any time she tried to swallow. Doctors inserted a feeding tube into her stomach.

She could still walk then, but she never consumed anything by mouth again. She spoke with guttural sounds, her hands moved in jerky, strained bursts—and she was angry. Who wouldn't be? I remember her face clouding over with fury. Sometimes she would complain with grunts and awkward swipes when her mother adjusted her bib.

I don't know what brought about the change. I can't even remember precisely when it happened, but over the years Carolyn stopped complaining. By the time her life ended at age twenty-seven, she glowed with sweetness. Though she could no longer walk or smile, she communicated love with her huge blue eyes.

On one of the last Sundays of her life, in a conservative church where no one raises his or her hands in worship, a movement from Carolyn prompted her father to glance her direction. Tears pooled in her eyes, and knotted hands quivered as they strained to reach heavenward in worship as her countenance glowed with adoration and love for Jesus. Not a complaining bone remained in my niece's ravaged body.

If anyone deserved to complain about life, Carolyn did. Instead, she chose acceptance and gratitude. I want an attitude like hers.

Why It Matters To You and Me

God created this world and everything in it. From the majesty of the mountains and sunsets down to every microscopic cell of the human body, creation displays his glory and power. It declares his love for us—because he made it all for us.

God did not create evil. Humanity invited it onto the scene in the Garden of Eden. God could have stopped it, of course, since he can do anything he wishes, but he didn't, because he had already given Adam the gift of free will.

Even after the fall, God didn't abandon us. He still sends down every good and perfect gift that reaches earth (see James 1:17). He even takes bad things that result from evil and uses them for his glory and our good. Like an artist crafting a rich tapestry, he takes the troubles we face and weaves them, along with the joys he sends, into a beautiful work of art. When we submit to him without complaining, we permit him to work unhindered, shaping us into unique people he cherishes. In us, his pure white light shines brighter when contrasted against the dark hues of suffering.

That's why God becomes very angry when we complain (see Deut. 1:34). Complaining accompanies hardness of heart and prevents God from working in us. If we complain enough, he may grant our requests, but he'll send leanness to our souls (see Ps. 106:15, KJV). Pray for your children to resist complaining so he can work in them.

Better yet, pray for the opposite of complaining. Ask God to encourage them to praise, no matter how difficult the circumstances. Shortly before my pastor died of leukemia, he told the congregation he had no desire to ask God why. Rather, he chose to offer God a sacrifice of praise by thanking him for his goodness and mercy. Pray for your children to follow his example.

Scripture Prayers You Can Pray for Your Children

- Many godless sinners are grumblers and complainers, doing whatever evil they feel like (see Jude 1:16). Please keep _____ from ever becoming like that.

- In everything _____ does, keep him [her] from complaining and arguing so that no one can speak a word of blame against him [her]. Help him [her] live a clean, innocent life as a child of God in a dark world full of crooked and perverse people. Let his [her] life shine brightly before them (see Phil. 2:14, 15).

- Don't let _____ forget that complaints are against you, not people (see Exod. 16:8).

- Remind _____ that when you hear complaining, you become very angry (see Deut. 1:34).

- Teach _____ not to grumble, as some of the Israelites did, for that's why you sent your angel of death to destroy them. Help him [her] understand that all those events happened to them as examples for us. They were written down to warn us, who live at this time when this age is drawing to a close (see 1 Cor. 10:10, 11).

Sharing My Thoughts with the Lord in Prayer

How this applies to my family and me

_____
_____
_____
_____
_____
_____
_____
_____
_____
_____
_____

My specific prayer for:

_____
_____
_____
_____
_____
_____
_____
_____

Insights received as I prayed

_____
_____
_____
_____
_____

What I believe God will do

_____
_____
_____
_____
_____
_____
_____

Watching for answers:

Date and answer

_____
_____
_____
_____

Date and answer

_____
_____
_____
_____

Date and answer

_____
_____
_____

Make Them Willing to Forgive

Why It Is Important

The year Sharon graduated from college, her sister, Kathy, ran away and married a man their parents despised. Six months later Sharon's father died of a heart attack, and Sharon blamed her sister. She vowed she would never forgive her. And she didn't.

It made no difference to her that Kathy's Christian marriage was a happy one and that their father had been wrong to oppose it. She didn't soften when Kathy asked for forgiveness and, over the years, tried again and again to mend their relationship. Inside the wall of hatred Sharon had built against her sister, tendrils of bitterness wrapped her in a viselike grip, squeezing the joy out of her life. She failed in every job she attempted but hated staying home. Anger rotted away her marriage and then moved on to her alienate her children. People who had known her as a bubbly twenty-year-old barely recognized the thin-lipped matron who made life miserable for everyone around her.

Sharon wanted to punish her sister by nurturing a grudge against her, but she damaged herself instead.

Why It Matters To You and Me

Forgiveness is at the core of the Christian faith. God set the ultimate example when he sent his Son to die so our sins could be forgiven. Since that was so difficult for him, he doesn't let us off the hook when forgiving is hard for us. He expects us to follow his example and forgive those who harm us. He's adamant about it.

Time after time in the Bible, God insists we must forgive the people who hurt us. He goes so far as to say, "If you forgive those who sin against you, your heavenly Father will forgive you. But if you refuse to forgive others, your Father will not forgive your sins" (Matt. 6:14–15). In the eighteenth chapter of Matthew, he calls the unforgiving servant evil and tosses him into jail.

God has good reasons for speaking so strongly about this issue:

- God wants the best for us. Every command in his Word is intended for our benefit—including his command to forgive. He knows that each person who refuses to forgive will suffer harm.

- God loves everyone, not just you and me. He desires for everyone to feel the relief and hope that follows forgiveness. He delights to see relationships restored when we forgive.

    - He longs for us to love him. We reveal the depth of our love when we follow his example and forgive others

- Few things hamper God's work more than lack of forgiveness. When Christians harbor grudges, the Holy Spirit can't move. Bitterness and resentment tie his hands.

Do you want peace and contentment for your children? Ask the Lord to show them that an unforgiving spirit is as much a sin as murder or immorality. Pray for them to give their desire for revenge to the Lord. Ask Jesus to help them stop stewing about how good things might be if the past were different.

Pray for them to be willing to forgive the people who wrong them so God won't be forced to discipline them. Pray for God's forgiving love to shine through them as an inspiration to everyone they meet.

Scripture Prayers You Can Pray for Your Children

- Help _____ never seek revenge or bear a grudge against anyone but to love her [his] neighbor as herself [himself]. You are the Lord (see Lev. 19:18).

- Forgive _____'s sins, just as he [she] forgives those who have sinned against him [her] (see Luke 11:4).

- Teach _____ to forgive those who sin against her [him], so that you will forgive her [him] (see Matt. 6:14).

- O God, thank you for forgiving all of _____'s sins. You canceled the record that contained the charges against her [him]. You took it and destroyed it by nailing it to Christ's cross (see Col. 2:13, 14).

- Teach _____ to be kind to others, tenderhearted, forgiving others, just as you through Christ Jesus have forgiven him [her] (see Eph. 4:32).

- Help _____ to forgive (for whatever is to be forgiven) so that Satan will not outsmart her [him] (see 2 Cor. 2:10, 11).

Sharing My Thoughts with the Lord in Prayer

How this applies to my Family and me

_____
_____
_____
_____
_____
_____
_____
_____
_____
_____
_____

My specific prayer for:

_____
_____
_____
_____
_____
_____
_____
_____
_____

Insights received as I prayed

_____
_____
_____
_____
_____
_____

What I believe God will do

_____
_____
_____
_____
_____
_____

Watching for answers:

Date and answer

_____
_____
_____
_____
_____

Date and answer

_____
_____
_____
_____
_____

Date and answer

_____
_____
_____
_____
_____

Keep Pride Out of
Their Hearts

Why It Is Important

My husband asked our son if he would work on the farm rather than seek a job away from home this summer. He needed Tevin's help roofing the house, replacing fences, hauling several tons of hay, and doing lots of odd jobs. Tev agreed. He didn't realize one of those odd jobs would entail refinishing several pieces of furniture out on the deck, a job he would not normally choose to do. He did an adequate job.

A couple days into the refinishing project, I chatted with Tevin and his sister while they worked on a puzzle after dinner. "I'm getting ready to write a chapter on pride," I told them. "Can either of you think of a good anecdote for me?"

Tevin leaned back in the maple chair, a bemused look on his face. "Yeah, I've got one about a kid named . . . let's see . . . you can call him . . . um . . . Kevin. Okay?" His eyes twinkled. "He had to refinish some furniture but wouldn't listen to his mother's instructions, because he didn't want to admit she knew more about it than he did. So he globbed on the finish too thickly, and that caused him lots of extra work."

We laughed together. I loved Tevin's story—not the one he told but the one he showed. Examples of pride are never far away, because we all struggle with that particular sin.

Why It Matters To You and Me

Pride was the first sin. Before God formed the earth, he created Satan, a mighty angelic guardian, the perfection of wisdom and beauty. God adorned him with gems set in gold—sapphires, turquoise, and emeralds. At first, Satan was blameless in all he did, but because of his beauty, pride corrupted his heart (see Ezek. 28:11–17). Consumed with that pride, he competed with God, and the Father cast him down to earth. Ever since his defeat, this monster has relentlessly striven to destroy the people of earth with the same sin that caused his downfall.

All evil seems to begin with the sin of pride. It appears first in the list of Sodom's sins. Glutted with pride, the city did loathsome things, and God wiped it out (see Ezek. 16:49–50). Pride still tempts our best and brightest. It lures many of our athletes into adultery, violence, and even murder. It sucks politicians into the sewer of deceit and outright theft.

We ordinary people aren't exempt. We succumb to pride way too often. How ironic that the blessings God pours out on us because he loves us are the very things we twist into pride! How sad that instead of giving God credit, we swell with pride, attributing achievements to our natural potential! We boast as though we're responsible for our own gifts.

Pray that your children will be confident and satisfied yet not hold an overly high opinion of themselves. Ask God to teach them to honestly evaluate themselves while they depend on him and understand that everything they have and are comes from him.

Scripture Prayers You Can Pray for Your Children

- Teach _____ that you despise pride. Assure him [her] that the proud will be punished (see Prov. 16:8).

- Protect _____ from the things the world offers, the lust for physical pleasure, the lust for everything we see, and pride in our possessions. These are not from you. They are from this evil world (see 1 John 2:16).

- Keep reminding _____ that you set yourself against the proud but show favor to the humble (see 1 Pet. 5:5).

- Don't let _____ forget that you scatter the proud and haughty ones (see Luke 1:51).

- Heavenly Father, don't let _____ be chosen as an elder while he [she] is a new Christian, because he [she] might be proud of being chosen so soon, and the devil will use that pride to make him [her] fall (see 1 Tim. 3:6).

- Remind _____, Lord, that though you are great and care for the humble, you keep your distance from the proud (see Ps. 138:6).

Sharing My Thoughts with the Lord in Prayer

How this applies to my family
and me

_____
_____
_____
_____
_____
_____
_____
_____
_____
_____

My specific prayer for:

_____
_____
_____
_____
_____
_____
_____
_____

Insights received as I prayed

_____
_____
_____
_____
_____

What I believe God will do

_____
_____
_____
_____
_____
_____
_____

Watching for answers:

Date and answer

_____
_____
_____
_____
_____

Date and answer

_____
_____
_____
_____
_____

Date and answer

_____
_____
_____
_____
_____

Praying for a Close Relationship with the Lord

Help Them Understand How Much God Loves Them

Why It Is Important

My beloved pastor Ron Mehl lived a life characterized by Jesus' love. During the twenty-three years he battled leukemia, though he often felt ill, he worked longer hours than most healthy people, shepherding the largest church in Oregon. He pushed himself because he understood Jesus' love more deeply than most of us, and he longed to share it with as many people as possible. Many times after suffering through miserable cancer treatments during the week, he would preach four sermons on Sunday, then travel around the world speaking to thousands the next week.

On one trip to China, he left his hotel room for an early-morning stroll. Not far from the hotel, a tiny elderly woman slept on the street under threadbare blankets. As he approached, she awakened and held up two withered palms, begging.

Pastor Ron lowered his six-foot-four-inch frame to kneel on the hard surface beside her. He emptied both pockets, giving her every cent he carried. Then, taking her hands in his, he began to weep. Because he couldn't speak her language, he had no way to share the love of Christ with her. He spent the next three days in his hotel room praying for the Lord to send someone to tell that precious woman how much Jesus loved her.

Because Pastor Ron loved Jesus so much, he loved people,

too. The love of Christ flowing through him made everyone who met him feel special.

Why It Matters To You and Me

We all need love. That's why reading the angel's words to Daniel always makes me weep. "'Don't be afraid,' he said, 'for you are deeply loved by God. Be at peace; take heart and be strong!'" (Dan. 10:10, emphasis added). I weep because I long to claim those words for myself, but I know I don't deserve the same kind of love Daniel did. Daniel was a special person. I'm not.

Yet hard as it is to believe, God loves me as deeply as he loved Daniel. And he loves my children, and you and your children, just as much. I know this because Jesus specifically mentioned us during his last hours on earth. He went to great lengths to specify exactly whom he loved: "I am praying not only for these disciples but also for all who will ever believe in me because of their testimony" (John 17:20). That's us! So we know he was referring to us as he continued, "Then the world will know that you sent me and will understand that you love them as much as you love me" (John 17:23, emphasis added).

Unbelievable! God loves you and your children as much as he loves Jesus, his precious Son. And Jesus loved you and your children enough to suffer and die on the Cross for you.

It's too much for us to fathom. That's why Paul told the Ephesians, "May you have the power to understand, as all God's people should, how wide, how long, how high, and how deep his love really is. May you experience the love of Christ, though it is so great you will never fully understand it" (Eph. 3:18, 19).

You and your children are deeply loved. Pray that you'll gain a greater and greater understanding of that love. Pray for the Lord to fill you with his love so that you, like Pastor Ron, will know how to pass it along to your children. Pray for your children to be certain of God's love—and yours—so they'll make others feel special.

Scripture Prayers You Can Pray for Your Children

- Help _____ love Jesus because Jesus first loved him [her] (see 1 John 4:19).

- Show _____ how to love you with all her [his] heart, soul, and strength (see Deut. 6:5).

- Teach _____ that if someone says, "I love God," but hates a Christian brother or sister, that person is a liar; for if we don't love people we can see, how can we love you, whom we have not seen? Remind her [him] that you yourself have commanded that we must love not only you but our Christian brothers and sisters too (see 1 John 4:20, 21).

- Help _____ obey the new commandment Jesus gave: "Love each other. Just as I have loved you, you should love each other. Your love for one another will prove to the world that you are my disciples" (John 13:34, 35).

- Encourage _____ and _____ to continue to love each other with true Christian love (see Heb. 13:1).

Sharing My Thoughts with the Lord in Prayer

How this applies to my family and me

_____
_____
_____
_____
_____
_____
_____
_____
_____
_____
_____

My specific prayer for:

_____
_____
_____
_____
_____
_____
_____
_____
_____

Insights received as I prayed

_____
_____
_____
_____
_____

What I believe God will do

_____
_____
_____
_____
_____
_____
_____

Watching for answers:

Date and answer

_____
_____
_____
_____
_____

Date and answer

_____
_____
_____
_____
_____

Date and answer

_____
_____
_____
_____

Protect My Children from False Gods

Why It Is Important

A young woman I know works in a facility for psychologically disturbed girls and boys aged fourteen to eighteen. She tells me that all but two of the twenty residents there embrace the Wiccan religion. These children cast spells, which resemble prayer, worship the moon and various other gods, and argue passionately that the sacrifice of innocent blood is good because it's intended to accomplish positive results. One girl openly refers to herself as a witch.

Recently a resident counselor at the facility brought in a Bible. When one of the girls stopped practicing Wicca and began to read it, her behavior improved markedly. Then she gave up reading the Bible, and her conduct deteriorated. My friend, who holds a degree in psychology, believes there's a definite connection between the religious beliefs of these children and the fact that they're severely mentally disturbed. She hopes to do research to prove it.

Why It Matters To You and Me

This seems like a pretty ridiculous topic for a prayer journal, doesn't it? Obviously, you're a Christian. You love the Lord. You're raising your kids right. There's no chance they would turn to other gods. Right?

Think again. In October 2002 the *Oregonian* newspaper ran stories about Wicca and Islam on two consecutive Sundays. The purpose was to explain why so many Americans are converting to those two rapidly growing religions. Six converts were featured in the articles, five of whom were former Christians, one from a Baptist pastor's family. Yet they had turned away from Jesus to worship other gods.

This is really nothing new. For years we've known that a high percentage of cult members come from Christian backgrounds. In 1978 over nine hundred followers of Jim Jones died in a mass suicide in Guyana, obeying him as though he were a god. Yet Jones started out as an ordained minister in a mainline Christian denomination, the Disciples of Christ.

I wish I could tell you how or why it happens, but I can only guess. Maybe these people grew tired of what they perceived as hypocritical behavior on the part of other Christians. Maybe peer pressure or persuasive college lectures drew them into error. Maybe they preferred the ease of a false religion. Maybe they were never firmly entrenched in the Christian belief system. No one knows for sure. We know only that though they once called themselves Christians, they turned to other gods.

I've seen it personally. I attended an Evangelical Christian church with Lorelei before I lost track of her for a couple of years. When I subsequently ran into her at a basketball game, she spoke animatedly about her new church. "It embraces all religions," she told me. "I get such a warm feeling there." She didn't seem to understand that Jehovah God insists we worship only him, or that Jesus states that he's the only way to the Father, or that Paul says that when we worship other gods we're actually worshiping demons (see 1 Cor. 10:19, 20). The last I heard of Lorelei, she had divorced, and her sixteen-year-old son had moved into an apartment by himself, stealing food from a grocery store in order to eat.

Following Jehovah God and his Son, Jesus, is the only way to heaven and the only path to blessing. We all need to pray that our children will never be tempted to worship false gods.

Scripture Prayers You Can Pray for Your Children

- Teach _____ there's only one God, you, the Father, who created everything, and that we exist for you. Show him [her] that there's only one Lord, Jesus Christ, through whom you made everything and through whom we have been given life (see 1 Cor. 8:6).

- Keep _____ from putting any other gods before you (see Deut. 5:7).

- Make _____ always follow hard after you, because people who chase after other gods will be filled with sorrow (see Ps. 16:4).

- Help _____ understand that if he [she] forsakes you and serves other gods, you will turn against him [her] and destroy him [her], even though you have been so good to him [her] (see Josh. 24:20).

- Teach _____ that before he [she] knew God, he [she] was a slave to so-called gods that don't even exist (see Gal. 4:8).

Sharing My Thoughts with the Lord in Prayer

How this applies to my family and me

_____
_____
_____
_____
_____
_____
_____
_____
_____
_____
_____

My specific prayer for:

_____
_____
_____
_____
_____
_____
_____
_____

Insights received as I prayed

_____
_____
_____
_____
_____

What I believe God will do

_____
_____
_____
_____
_____
_____
_____

Watching for answers:

Date and answer

_____
_____
_____
_____

Date and answer

_____
_____
_____
_____
_____

Date and answer

_____
_____
_____
_____

Don't Let Them
Grieve Your Spirit

Why It Is Important

You rent movies once in a while, right? Well, let's imagine this is one of your movie nights. You've already popped the corn and poured sodas. Everyone finds a comfortable seat, and you start the movie. It's R-rated for sexual content and language. You feel a twinge of guilt about that, but all videos have a little nudity and a few swear words these days.

About halfway through the movie, a steamy part fills the screen. You hear a sound and look up in time to see Jesus enter the room. You glance over and greet him with a friendly smile. "Lord! Good to see you! Have a seat." It's nice of him to visit—too bad you don't have time to chat right now.

Jesus lowers himself onto the sofa, sorrowful eyes fixed on the screen. The scene changes, and someone makes an off-color joke. When you laugh, a couple of tears slip from Jesus' eyes, but you're too engrossed in the show to notice. Every time his Father's name is used in vain on the screen, Jesus cringes.

I know you're thinking this sounds ridiculous. But maybe it isn't as ridiculous as you think. Though Jesus doesn't physically walk on this earth, when you accepted the Lord, the spirit of Christ came to live inside you. He's with you all the time. Everything you see Jesus is forced to see, just as surely as if he were sitting beside you on the couch. You compel him to look at things that make him sick. Movies are just one very small example.

Everything you say and hear, he must endure—because he sees and hears it right along with you. Think of all the times you tell small lies, hurt the feelings of coworkers, gossip, slander—the list goes on and on. He even hears your negative thoughts. Because he loves and refuses to leave you, he suffers every time you choose evil. And he's much more sensitive to evil than we are.

Why It Matters To You and Me

You children mirror you. They think thoughts they shouldn't. They spew angry, put-down comments at each other. For the most part, they don't even notice their bad behavior. It's part of the human condition. Through constant exposure, we get so accustomed to evil that we barely notice it.

But Jesus does. His Holy Spirit never hardens to evil the way we do when we're exposed to it repeatedly. He feels fresh pain every time we make wrong choices—even though he understands we don't mean to deliberately hurt him. He knows we just don't get it. He understands that some part of us can't comprehend that he's actually living inside us. We behave badly and foster sinful attitudes because we aren't sensitive to him. We forget he experiences everything we experience.

Pray for your children to keep an awareness of his presence and a sensitivity to him. Pray for them to gain an increased understanding of what the Holy Spirit is doing for them. Pray they'll feel deep gratitude for the sacrifices he makes in staying with them every minute of every day. Ask God to help your children understand that the Holy Spirit loves them so much he'll never leave them, even though living inside them often causes him great pain.

Scripture Prayers You Can Pray for Your Children

- Father, thank you for sending the Counselor as Jesus' representative—and by the Counselor I mean the Holy Spirit. Thank you that he will teach _____ everything and will remind him [her] of everything Jesus told us (see John 14:26).

- Never let _____ forget that the Spirit of Christ lives within him [her]. Even though his [her] body may die because of sin, his [her] spirit is alive because he [she] has been made right with you. Your Spirit, who raised Jesus from the dead, lives in him [her] (see Rom. 8:10, 11).

- Remind _____ that her [his] body is the temple of the Holy Spirit, who lives in her [him] and was given to her [him] by you (see 1 Cor. 6:19)

- Keep _____ from ever bringing sorrow to your Holy Spirit by the way he [she] lives. Help him [her] remember that the Holy Spirit is the one who has identified him [her] as his own, guaranteeing that he [she] will be saved on the day of redemption (see Eph. 4:30).

- With the help of the Holy Spirit, who lives within us, help _____ carefully guard what has been entrusted to him [her] (see 2 Tim. 1:14).

Sharing My Thoughts with the Lord in Prayer

How this applies to my family and me

_____
_____
_____
_____
_____
_____
_____
_____
_____

My specific prayer for:

_____
_____
_____
_____
_____
_____
_____
_____

Insights received as I prayed

_____
_____
_____
_____
_____

What I believe God will do

_____
_____
_____
_____
_____
_____

Watching for answers:

Date and answer

_____
_____
_____
_____

Date and answer

_____
_____
_____
_____
_____

Date and answer

_____
_____
_____
_____

Teach Them It Is Okay to Ask

Why It Is Important

A year ago my cousin Jim had a heart attack and a stroke. I'm not quite certain which happened first. The heart attack left him with only twenty-percent heart function and in need of a transplant. The stroke paralyzed his right side. Grading papers for the Internet classes he teaches then took longer because he had to do all the work using only one hand. Still, he rarely complained. Instead, he read the Bible and scoured Christian books to learn more about the Lord.

Recently, I felt a strong urge to call my cousin. I thought it was from God, though I wasn't certain. So I phoned him. "I'm going blind," Jim told me. "I can't see to read. I can't teach my classes. I don't have any way to support myself. Jeannie, I can handle the rest of my disabilities, but I don't know how to be a blind man, too." Before we hung up, I prayed for him.

The next week Jim called to tell me the Lord touched his eyes a couple of days after we prayed over the phone. His vision still was not perfect—he would need new glasses—but the recent blurred sight and double vision had disappeared. Praise God!

God loves my cousin. He wanted to touch my cousin. I believe he prompted me to call Jim because he knew I would ask him to touch him.

Why It Matters To You and Me

My mother always cautioned me never to ask for candy when visiting someone's house. She warned me so strongly that I still have trouble accepting gifts. I passed the philosophy on to my children. Maybe your parents taught you the same thing. I wonder if that's why we're so shy about asking God for favors. We think it's impolite.

Not only is it okay for you to ask God for whatever you need—he wants you to. He wants you to ask him to give your children wonderful lives, draw them to his love, and heal them from physical and emotional pain. It's all right to ask him for help as they take tests or to supply a fantastic future mate. He wants you to ask for wisdom as you discipline them. When things go wrong, he wants to hear about every detail from you. He wants you do admit you can't fix it and then ask him to make things better.

I think it's even okay to ask for an expensive jacket for your daughter or for God to help your son shoot twenty points in a basketball game. He just may give you those things. He wants to bless you and your children.

Hours before Jesus gave his life for us, he repeatedly encouraged his disciples to ask:

- "You can ask for anything in my name, and I will do it, because the work of the Son brings glory to the Father. Yes, ask anything in my name, and I will do it!" (John 14:13, 14).

- "If you stay joined to me and my words remain in you, you may ask any request you like, and it will be granted!" (John 15:7).

- Ask, using my name, and you will receive, and you will have abundant joy (John 16:24).

After Jesus died and rose, his younger brother reinforced his words: "The reason you don't have what you want is that you don't ask God for it. And even when you do ask, you don't get it because your whole motive is wrong—you want only what will give you pleasure" (James 4:2, 3).

Make many requests for yourself and your children that are in line with God's Word and will. Not only will the results please you—they'll please Jesus, too.

Scripture Prayers You Can Pray for Your Children

- Teach _____ to ask with right motives—not just for things that will give her [him] pleasure (see James 4:3).

- Show _____ that she [he] can go directly to you and ask you, and you will grant her [his] request because she [he] uses Jesus' name (see John 16:23).

- Convince _____ that she [he] can ask you in Jesus' name, for you love her [him] dearly because she [he] loves Jesus and believes that he came from you (see John 16:26, 27).

- Help _____ keep on asking, and he [she] will be given what he [she] asks for. Show him [her] how to keep on looking, and he [she] will find. Make him [her] keep on knocking, and the door will be opened (see Matt. 7:7).

- Make _____ confident that you will listen to her [him] whenever she [he] asks you for anything in line with your will. Teach her [him] that you will be listening when she [he] makes her [his] requests, and she [he] can be sure that you will give her [him] what she [he] asks for (see 1 John 5:14, 15).

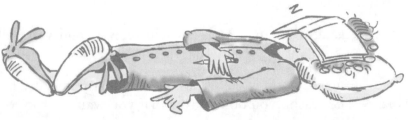

Sharing My Thoughts with the Lord in Prayer

How this applies to my family
and me

_____
_____
_____
_____
_____
_____
_____
_____
_____
_____

My specific prayer for:

_____
_____
_____
_____
_____
_____
_____
_____

Insights received as I prayed

_____
_____
_____
_____

What I believe God will do

_____
_____
_____
_____
_____
_____
_____

Watching for answers:

Date and answer

_____
_____
_____
_____
_____

Date and answer

_____
_____
_____
_____
_____

Date and answer

_____
_____
_____
_____
_____

Praying for Relationships

Help Them Find
Top-Quality Friends

Why It Is Important

When a godly person develops a close relationship with a person of weak character, the bad person often pulls the good one down. Rarely does the influence of the good person elevate the bad person. It's been that way since the beginning of time. The apostle Paul quotes a third-century B.C. writer who says everyone knows "bad company corrupts good character" (see 1 Cor. 15:33). Though you can probably think of a story to illustrate that point, I'd like to share two very sad ones with you:

Keely grew up in a parsonage, attended Christian college, then wowed everyone in a large church with her energy and talents. After two years, when that job no longer fulfilled her, she headed across the country to pursue her dream of becoming an artist. At art school, she shared an apartment with a girl whose morals and beliefs differed radically from hers. I can't explain how or why the close friendship with her roommate and a few other university students gradually changed Keely's values, but they did. By the end of art school, she was dancing nude and living with her boyfriend.

The second story is at least as tragic. Everyone at the Christian school loved Bryant. He was the perfect student and friend. He loved and protected his younger brother, Jayson. Even when Jayson fell in with the wrong crowd and began using drugs, Bryant sided with him. After Jayson's dealer murdered him, Bryant pushed his way into court and tried to avenge his brother by stabbing the murderer. Just as bad companions corrupted Jayson, excusing his brother's bad actions changed Bryant's good values. Bryant now serves time in prison.

Why It Matters To You and Me

We all need relationships. God himself said so in Genesis when he declared, "It is not good for the man to be alone" (Gen. 2:18). When God spoke those words, he referred to more than marriage. Human beings need other human beings. Your children need friends. Your job is to guide them in choosing good ones—friends who will inspire them to excellence.

Observe your children carefully. If you notice one of them picking friends with weak character, discuss it with them. Don't be afraid of offending. Explain to your child why you consider that particular friend an unwise choice. Then pray for the Lord make your child willing to listen to your sound advice.

I'm not suggesting your children avoid all people who are not Christians. They should reach out to people who don't know the Lord, of course. God expects them to be friendly and available to help classmates and coworkers. But they should relate to those individuals on a different level than they do with close friends. Their best friends, the kids with whom they spend the majority of their time and whose opinions they value, should be of high moral character.

Troublemakers and hot-tempered people should be kept at arms' length. My husband, a former criminal investigator for the federal government, could spend hours regaling you with stories of good people who ended up in prison after joining up with bad people. Unequally yoked friendships and partnerships can cause misery and suffering.

It's our responsibility as parents to teach our children the importance of choosing friends with character. It's better for the ones we love so deeply to endure loneliness rather than partner with someone who might damage their values. We need to prepare our sons and daughters for the possibility of standing alone during times when godly friends can't be found. These times will be temporary. As you pray, God will ease the loneliness and help your children seek out godly friends.

Scripture Prayers You Can Pray for Your Children

- Keep _____ away from angry, short-tempered people, or he [she] will learn to be like them and endanger his [her] soul (see Prov. 22:24, 25).

- Teach _____ to walk with the wise so she [he] will become wise. Don't let her [him] walk with fools, or she [he] will suffer harm (see Prov. 13:20).

- Lord, make _____ turn his [her] back if sinners entice him [her]. Keep him [her] from going along with those who say, "Come and join us. Let's hide and kill someone! Let's ambush the innocent! Let's swallow them alive as the grave swallows its victims. Though they are in the prime of life, they will go down into the pit of death. And the loot we'll get! We'll fill our houses with all kinds of things! Come on, throw in your lot with us; we'll split our loot with you." Keep him [her] far away from their paths (see Prov. 1:10–15).

- Like David, help _____ not tolerate people who slander their neighbors. Keep her [him] from close friendships with people filled with conceit and pride (see Ps. 101:5).

- Help _____ never team up with those who are unbelievers. How can goodness be a partner with wickedness? How can light live with darkness? What harmony can there be between Christ and the devil? How can a believer partner with an unbeliever? (see 2 Cor. 6:14, 15).

Sharing My Thoughts with the Lord in Prayer

How this applies to my family and me

_____
_____
_____
_____
_____
_____
_____
_____
_____
_____

My specific prayer for:

_____
_____
_____
_____
_____
_____
_____
_____

Insights received as I prayed

_____
_____
_____
_____
_____

What I believe God will do

_____
_____
_____
_____
_____
_____

Watching for answers:

Date and answer

_____
_____
_____
_____

Date and answer

_____
_____
_____
_____

Date and answer

_____
_____
_____
_____

Establish Them in a Church Family

Why It Is Important

Have you ever participated in a wave at a sporting event? There's something thrilling about it, isn't there? Thousands of fans who have never met before unify to show support for the guys on the field. Wow! It feels good, even when you're just watching it on television.

That's what I imagine Sunday morning church looks like from heaven. I can see Jesus gazing down from the window of heaven, elbows on the sill, chin propped on two fists, beaming with joy. He watches the sunrise encircle the earth, and as it moves, believers in churches around the world stand to salute him in a lavish global wave of worship and praise. Then a hush descends as they listen to teachings about him. He has to love it.

Why It Matters To You and Me

I don't know how many times I've heard the question, usually spoken in a mildly hostile tone: "Do you have to go to church to be a Christian?" The answer is an obvious and emphatic "no." The faith of untold millions of Christians has grown stronger when adversaries of Christ prevented them from meeting together. Those locked in solitary confinement because of their beliefs enjoyed an especially close relationship with Jesus.

A better question might be "Why wouldn't I want to go to God's house?" Most of those imprisoned saints were thrown in jail precisely because they tried to gather with other believers. God himself came up with the idea of believers gathering to worship him. In the Old Testament he commanded his children to revere him as a community, first at the Tent of Meeting and later at the Temple in Jerusalem. Often Israelites walked many miles to attend those meetings, but it was worth it. A choir of five thousand praised Jehovah to the accompaniment of trumpets, harps, and cymbals. Priests offered sacrifices to the Lord, and everyone enjoyed a sumptuous meal in his honor. Sometimes the glorious presence of God manifested in a shining cloud.

In the New Testament, God's desire for Christians to worship corporately remained constant. The apostle Paul commands us not to forsake gathering together (see Heb. 10:25).

We're the living stones of God's temple. As a group, we teach the Word, provide fellowship for believers, and share the gospel with non-believers. We can even afford to feed the hungry and send missionaries to the far corners of the earth. We stand as the family of God, a witness to the world. When we join in perfect unity, we do mighty works that none of us can accomplish in isolation.

On an individual level, only a few close friends are necessary when life flows along smoothly, but times of difficulty require more people. We need God's bigger family to help shoulder our burdens. Like iron sharpening iron, those family members call us to responsibility, keeping us on the right path. They encourage us to good works. And we do the same for them. God commands us to gather together so he can bless us with the gift of one another. Your children need the church.

Pray for them to find a welcoming church filled with God's Holy Spirit. Ask the Lord to teach your kids how to reach out to other members of God's family, being included and including others. Pray for the church to shine as a living, growing body that knows the truth of the Scriptures and how to worship and pray effectively.

Scripture Prayers You Can Pray for Your Children

- Help _____ think of ways to encourage others to outbursts of love and good deeds. And don't let her [him] neglect meeting with other believers, as some people do (see Heb. 10:24, 25).

- Lord, show _____ that we're all one body. We have the same Spirit, and we have all been called to the same glorious future. Always keep us united in the Holy Spirit and bound together in peace (see Eph. 4:3, 4).

- Keep _____ connected to Christ, the head of the Body. Show him [her] that we're all joined together in Christ's body by his strong sinews (see Col. 2:19).

- Remind _____ that you're building all believers as living stones into your spiritual temple (see 1 Pet. 2:5).

- Show _____ how wonderful it is, how pleasant, when brothers and sisters live together in unity (see Ps. 133:1).

- Convince _____ that as our bodies have many parts and each part has a special function, so it is with Christ's body. We are all parts of his one body, and each of us has different work to do. And since we are all one body in Christ, we belong to each other, and each of us needs all the others (see Rom. 12:4, 5).

Sharing My Thoughts with the Lord in Prayer

How this applies to my family and me

_____
_____
_____
_____
_____
_____
_____
_____

My specific prayer for:

_____
_____
_____
_____
_____
_____

Insights received as I prayed

_____
_____
_____
_____

What I believe God will do

_____
_____
_____
_____

Watching for answers:

Date and answer

_____
_____
_____
_____

Date and answer

_____
_____
_____
_____

Date and answer

_____
_____
_____
_____

Keep Them Pure

Why It Is Important

An usher led me down the aisle that separated rows of white chairs facing a wooden platform. I took my seat with the other guests, listening to the murmur of their conversation, breathing in the fragrance of the pink roses that clambered over a trellis beside the platform. Nearby, a stream meandered around flowerbeds and emptied into a pond of water lilies. The setting was perfect.

Right on time, the music began. The bride, gorgeous in her long white dress of satin, lace, and pearls, strolled across a small arched bridge, holding her father's arm. A gentle breeze blew a loose strand of hair across her sun-dappled skin. The bride's father kissed her cheek and offered her hand to the groom, who was as handsome as the bride was beautiful. They looked breathtaking together.

The ceremony began. The couple smiled adoringly into each other's eyes, pledging their eternal love, promising to grow old together. Then in lieu of a prayer and the lighting of the unity candle, the couple turned toward the audience, and the wedding official spoke: "Ladies and gentlemen, the bride and groom wish to announce that this ceremony does not mark the beginning of their life together. It celebrates the continuation of an ongoing relationship that began over five years ago."

Rather than feeling ashamed of the fact that they had lived together for five years before marrying, they proudly proclaimed it in front of family, friends—and God.

Two years later they divorced.

Why It Matters To You and Me

Over one-third of people in the United States who marry get divorced. You knew that, right? But did you know that *Focus on the Family Magazine* says the divorce rate jumps to seventy-five percent for couples who live together before they marry? (Neil Clark Warren "The Cohabitation Epidemic," http://www.family.org/fof-mag/marriage/a0026415.cfm 2003)

Of course, that counts only couples who actually end up marrying. How many more suffer the trauma of a breakup without ever having formalized their relationship?

Only a few years ago, people who lived together outside of marriage were shunned by society. Sadly, the majority of our society no longer disapproves of the practice. Today, one out of every three adults has cohabited with someone of the opposite sex during their single years (Warren, "The Cohabitation Epidemic"). Nearly half of adults under thirty-five have lived with someone (Warren, "The Cohabitation Epidemic").

Emotional scars result when we brazenly break God's laws. And the Bible lists immorality as one of the most damaging sins. The hurt we carry from one fractured relationship into the next makes the new union more difficult.

However, there's hope for your children. The percentage of born-again Christians who have cohabited is lower than that for any other group: twenty-five percent (Warren, "The Cohabitation Epidemic"). If your children have a strong relationship with the Lord, they're less likely to fall into sexual sin.

Let your children see you holding firm in your stance against sex outside marriage, and then pray every day for them to remain sexually pure. Pray for them to resist the seductive images flashing from television and theatre screens. Ask the Lord to keep society's acceptance of sexual sin from seeping into their hearts. Pray for God to retain his position as the major influence in their lives.

Scripture Prayers You Can Pray for Your Children

- Don't let _____ spend any more of her [his] life chasing after evil desires, but make her [him] anxious to do your will. Thank you that she [he] has had enough in the past of the evil things that godless people enjoy—their immorality and lust, their feasting and drunkenness and wild parties (see 1 Pet. 4:3).

- Help _____ never forget the cities of Sodom and Gomorrah and their neighboring towns, which were filled with sexual immorality and every kind of sexual perversion. Those cities were destroyed by fire and are a warning of the eternal fire that will punish all who are evil (see Jude 7).

- Convince _____ that those who brazenly violate your will blaspheme you. Since they have treated your Word with contempt and deliberately disobeyed your commands, they must suffer the consequences of their guilt (see Num. 15:30, 31).

- Show _____ that we should be decent and true in everything we do so that everyone can approve of our behavior. Don't let him [her] participate in wild parties and getting drunk, or in adultery and immoral living, or in fighting jealousy. But let the Lord Jesus Christ take control of him [her]. Don't let him [her] even think of ways to indulge his [her] evil desires (see Rom. 13:13, 14).

- Remind _____ that Jesus said evil thoughts, murder, adultery, all other sexual immorality, theft, lying, and slander come from the heart and are the things that defile us (see Matt. 15:19, 20).

Sharing My Thoughts with the Lord in Prayer

How this applies to my family and me

_____
_____
_____
_____
_____
_____
_____
_____
_____
_____
_____

My specific prayer for:

_____
_____
_____
_____
_____
_____
_____
_____

Insights received as I prayed

_____
_____
_____
_____
_____
_____

What I believe God will do

_____
_____
_____
_____
_____
_____

Watching for answers:

Date and answer

_____
_____
_____
_____

Date and answer

_____
_____
_____
_____
_____

Date and answer

_____
_____
_____
_____

Bless My Children's Future Mates

Why It Is Important

It's difficult for me to comprehend the fact that my children's future mates are actual flesh-and-blood people who already exist. Some part of me imagines that they'll suddenly materialize from nothing, all grown-up and mature, just weeks before my children meet them—rather like Athena springing full grown from Zeus's forehead. I know better, of course. My future son-in-law and daughters-in-law do exist, and have for several years now. They are normal kids living in regular families with parents who love them but make mistakes.

Curiosity about them overwhelms me sometimes, just as it did about my own children before their births. With my own children, I wondered if they would have all their fingers and toes. I don't care so much about physical characteristics anymore. I'll take a three-toed daughter-in-law with character over a spoiled Miss Universe any day. I don't mind if they're hotties so my kids will be pleased, but looks don't concern me so much. I want to know about the more important things: Are they hard workers? Considerate? Loving and faithful? Are they humble yet confident in the Lord? Do they pray and read their Bibles every day? Do they have a deep commitment to the Lord?

My oldest son tells me he sees no reason to get married unless he finds a woman who is sold out to the Lord—one who is obviously on fire for God. Even though I want grandchildren, I agree with him. It would be better for him to remain single than marry the wrong person. The purpose of marriage is to reflect Christ and the Church, to make the unified pair more like Jesus than either would be alone—and to produce godly children.

A great marriage can accomplish all that. I want great marriages for my children. I know you want the same thing.

Why It Matters To You and Me

The divorce rate among born-again Christians is now statistically identical to the rate among non-Christian adults. George Barna reported in August 2001 that thirty-three percent of all born-again persons have experienced divorce, and ninety percent of them divorced after accepting Christ, not before ("Born Again Adults Less Likely to Co-habit, Just as Likely to Divorce" Barna Research Online, www.barna.org, Aug. 6, 2001). I don't understand why that would happen, but I know what it means to you and me. No one is immune, not even our precious children.

If I want my children to have great marriages, not only should I pray for my future son-in-law and daughters-in-law, but I should also pray wisdom and strength for their parents. My sons' future in-laws need wisdom as they discipline my sons' future wives. I should ask the Lord to give my daughter's future in-laws a strong marriage their son can emulate. I should start praying for that as soon as possible.

We need to ask the Lord to call our sons-in-law and daughters-in-law to himself, whether or not their parents know him. We need to beg the Lord to give all our children a commitment to purity—a strong determinations to stay abstinent until they marry. We should pray for the Lord to strengthen their character until they become godly people who walk worthy of him.

Despite the discouraging statistics, I believe good marriages are possible, and the most fulfilling marriages are between two godly people. That's why we need to start praying for our future children now and keep on praying right through the engagement, the honeymoon, and the birth of our grandchildren. The commitment to pray for our children's marriages should end only as we take our last breath.

Actually, you can stop then if you want to—but I intend to keep on talking to Jesus about it after I get to heaven.

Scripture Prayers You Can Pray for Your Children

- I pray for _____ and her [his] future husband [wife]. I give thanks to you, the Father of our Lord Jesus Christ, for I believe they will trust in Christ Jesus and will love all your people (see Col. 1:3, 4).

- Teach _____ and his [her] future wife [husband] to live in a way that will always honor and please you. Lead them to continually do good, kind things for others. All the while, help them learn to know you better and better (see Col. 1:10).

- Help _____ and her [his] future mate put to death the sinful, earthly things lurking within them so they will have nothing to do with sexual sin, impurity, lust, and shameful desires (see Col. 3:5).

- Since you have chosen _____ and _____ to be the holy people whom you love, help them clothe themselves with tenderhearted mercy, kindness, humility, gentleness and patience (see Col. 3:12).

- Please give _____ and his [her] future wife [husband] peace and love with faith, from you, the Father, and the Lord Jesus Christ. Let your grace be upon them because they love our Lord Jesus Christ with an undying love (see Eph. 6:23, 24).

Sharing My Thoughts with the Lord in Prayer

How this applies to my family
and me

_____
_____
_____
_____
_____
_____
_____
_____
_____
_____
_____

My specific prayer for:

_____
_____
_____
_____
_____
_____
_____
_____

Insights received as I prayed

_____
_____
_____
_____
_____

What I believe God will do

_____
_____
_____
_____
_____
_____

Watching for answers:

Date and answer

_____
_____
_____
_____

Date and answer

_____
_____
_____
_____

Date and answer

_____
_____
_____
_____

Praying God's Best for Our Children

Bring Them into Your Family

Why It Is Important

There's a myth in the Christian community that says believers are sweeter, kinder, and gentler than non-believers. I wish that were true. It should be—but it just isn't.

I have acquaintances who are believers as well as acquaintances who are non-believers. The believers are thoughtful and considerate, but so are the non-Christians. Both groups love their families and live moral lives. Sometimes it's hard to tell the difference between the two groups. Occasionally the non-believers rush to help someone in trouble more quickly than the believers do.

And that's the source of a dangerous myth among non-Christians—if you're a really good person, you'll go to heaven when you die. I wish that were true. But it just isn't.

A couple of years ago, in one month's time, my husband and I attended the funerals of two cherished friends. Both men died unexpectedly; both were professionals who tirelessly helped others. Neither, to my knowledge, acknowledged Jesus as Lord of his life.

Yet speakers at both services assured mourners the men were in heaven. I longed to believe them. I found myself thinking, They must be in heaven. How could God keep such good men out? I couldn't bear the thought of either of them in hell. Yet I'll be surprised to see either of them in heaven. Tragically, since they didn't want Jesus in their lives on earth, he won't force them to live with him through eternity. He grants us free will. We get what we choose.

Why It Matters To You and Me

Have you noticed that nearly everyone thinks he or she is going to heaven? Even the Columbine High School killers spoke of "going to a better place" while filming their basement pre-massacre video!

That idea is found nowhere in the Bible. Jesus said, "You can enter God's Kingdom only through the narrow gate. The highway to hell is broad, and its gate is wide for the many who choose the easy way. But the gateway to life is small, and the road is narrow, and only a few ever find it" (Matt 7:13, 14).

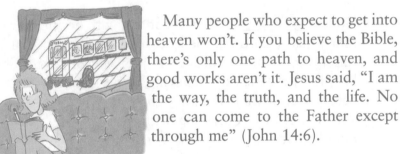

Many people who expect to get into heaven won't. If you believe the Bible, there's only one path to heaven, and good works aren't it. Jesus said, "I am the way, the truth, and the life. No one can come to the Father except through me" (John 14:6).

Because it is incomprehensible to think our children could miss heaven, the most important thing we can pray for is their salvation. Nothing else matters as much—not popularity, not grades, not wealth. When compared to eternity, your children's earthly achievements mean nothing. This life is brief. Life after death is forever, and your children will spend it in heaven or hell. There are no other options.

Pray, pray, pray until your children accept Jesus into their hearts.

Scripture Prayers You Can Pray for Your Children

- Teach _____ that if he [she] tries to keep his [her] life for himself [herself], he [she] will lose it. But if he [she] gives up his [her] life for your sake and for the sake of the Good News, he [she] will find true life. How does he [she] benefit if he [she] gains the whole world but loses his [her] own soul in the process? Nothing is worth more than his [her] soul (see Mark 8:35-37).

- Convince _____ that all have sinned, that all fall short of your glorious standard (see Rom. 3:23).

- Heavenly Father, make _____ right in your sight by her [his] trusting Jesus Christ to take away her [his] sins. Teach her [him] we can all be saved in this same way, no matter who we are or what we've done (see Rom. 3:22).

- God, if _____ will confess with her [his] mouth that Jesus is Lord and believe in her [his] heart that you raised him from the dead, she [he] will be saved. Show her [him] that it's by believing in her [his] heart that she [he] is made right with you and that it's by confessing with her [his] mouth that she [he] is saved (see Rom. 10:9, 10).

- Show _____ that the salvation that comes from trusting Christ—which is the message Paul preached—is already within easy reach. In fact, the Scriptures say, "The message is close at hand; it is on your lips and in your heart" (see Rom. 10:8).

Sharing My Thoughts with the Lord in Prayer

How this applies to my family and me

_____
_____
_____
_____
_____
_____
_____
_____
_____

My specific prayer for:

_____
_____
_____
_____
_____
_____
_____
_____

Insights received as I prayed

_____
_____
_____
_____
_____

What I believe God will do

_____
_____
_____
_____
_____
_____

Watching for answers:

Date and answer

_____
_____
_____
_____

Date and answer

_____
_____
_____
_____

Date and answer

_____
_____
_____
_____
_____

Teach My Children to Recognize God's Will

Why It Is Important

Four days after college graduation, Brandon landed a great job with a prestigious company in his hometown. Six months later, convinced that God couldn't possibly expect him to work the sixty hours per week required by his employer, he quit. He kicked back for a few weeks, hanging with friends and playing video games, and then hit the Internet in search of a new job.

The problem was that the economy had taken an unexpected downturn, and no one wanted to hire him. Brandon made call after call, doing his best to find another job. Nothing happened. When he sought the Lord's will through prayer and Bible study, it felt as though his prayers were banging against the ceiling. Why wouldn't the Lord answer him? The job search gradually petered out until he finally tried only sporadically to land one. He no longer followed up on job leads friends and family members offered.

Brandon felt worthless. Depression settled in. He anesthetized himself with computer video games, playing with friends late into the night, then sleeping through the afternoons. Obviously God intended better things for him, but he had no idea how to find God's will.

If your child were in Brandon's situation, would he or she be able to understand what God wanted him or her to do?

Why It Matters To You and Me

One of the most important things we parents can do is teach our children how to follow God's plan for their lives. That may seem complex and mysterious. It isn't.

God views his will for us a little differently than we tend to. He created us to glorify him and give him pleasure. He's in the business of forming us into his image. So he's most interested in developing our relationship with him as he shapes our character. When we think about God's will, we worry most about where God wants us to be. He's concerned more about what we're becoming.

Obedience to God is the key to becoming what he wants us to be. We must obey him if we're to walk in his will, and the only place we can discover what he wants us to do is his Word.

Rule: God's will is spelled out across the pages of the Bible. If you conform your choices to the instructions in his Word, daily striving to obey him, you will live in his will and be successful.

It's that simple. Conversely, every time we refuse to obey the Word, we step out of God's will. James 1:22, 23 tells us, "Remember, it is a message to obey, not just to listen to. If you don't obey, you are only fooling yourself. For if you just listen and don't obey, it is like looking at your face in a mirror but doing nothing to improve your appearance." Verse 25 promises God's blessing when we continue to read the Bible and do what it says.

Let's look at Brandon's situation. Though he was a Christian and studied God's Word, he didn't always obey it. Prov. 20:18 says we should seek wise advice. 2 Thess. 3:6 tells Christians to work hard. Ps. 90:12 says to make the most of our time. Isa. 40:31 instructs us to wait on the Lord. When Brandon violated those commands, he took himself out of God's will and opened the door for Satan to attack him with feelings of worthlessness.

If you want your children to walk in God's will, you must teach them the importance of reading, understanding, and obeying his Word; and then pray for him to give them a desire to do those things. As you keep praying for them to listen to God, he will reveal the path he has chosen for them.

Scripture Prayers You Can Pray for Your Children

- Lead _____ to acknowledge you in all her [his] ways, and you will direct her [his] paths (see Prov. 3:6, NKJV).

- Lord God, teach my children to obey your commands and walk in your ways; then you will establish them as your holy people (see Deut. 28:9).

- Lord, help _____ trust in you and do good. Then he [she] will live safely in the land and prosper. Help him [her] take delight in you, and you will give him [her] his [her] heart's desires. Teach him [her] to commit everything he [she] does to you, Lord. Enable him [her] to trust you. You will help him [her] (see Ps. 37:3–5).

- Lord, remind _____ that you promised your children, "Obey me, and I will be your God, and you will be my people. Only do as I say, and all will be well!" (see Jer. 7:23).

- Prompt _____ to call to you. You will answer, and show her [him] great and mighty things, which she [he] does not know (see Jer. 33:3, NKJV).

Sharing My Thoughts with the Lord in Prayer

How this applies to my family and me

_____
_____
_____
_____
_____
_____
_____
_____
_____
_____

My specific prayer for:

_____
_____
_____
_____
_____
_____
_____
_____

Insights received as I prayed

_____
_____
_____
_____
_____

What I believe God will do

_____
_____
_____
_____
_____
_____

Watching for answers:

Date and answer

_____
_____
_____
_____

Date and answer

_____
_____
_____
_____

Date and answer

_____
_____
_____
_____

Bless My Children and Grant the Desires of Their Hearts

Why It Is Important

My parents pastored churches for over forty years. More than once, when two churches called them at the same time, they struggled with knowing how to choose between the two congregations. They desired to serve where God wanted them and prayed for him to show them his will, but he seldom sent a clear answer. Once, on the advice of an older, wiser pastor, they accepted a cut in pay and the smaller of two churches. They enjoyed the time there so much that they knew had made the right choice. Another time, the churches seemed comparable and even their mentor-pastor couldn't discern what God intended for them. That's when the Lord showed my parents the David-Nathan principle.

David longed to build a temple for God. So he called Nathan, the prophet, to his palace and asked for God's permission to construct it. Nathan said, "Go ahead with what you have in mind, for God is with you" (1 Chr. 17:2). But later that night, God informed Nathan he had made an error. God planned to give David something different, something greater than David could have ever dreamed or imagined. Rather than David building a house for the Lord, God himself would build a house for David—an eternal dynasty that would include Jesus Christ himself.

My parents understood the "rule to live by" in that text: If you're walking in obedience to God's commands and listening for his instructions, follow your heart's desire unless he definitely gives you other instructions.

God wants to grant our desires, because if we're seeking him diligently, he's the one who placed those desires in our hearts in the first place. He'll stop us if we start to get off track. And when he stops us, it's because he has something better for us in the future.

Why It Matters To You and Me

God's fatherly love far outshines your love for your children. He longs to bless them. He wants to grant the desires of their hearts.

Matt. 7:11 says, "If you sinful people know how to give good gifts to your children, how much more will your heavenly Father give good gifts to those who ask him." God wants to give your children gifts you can't give them. James 1:17 tells us, "Whatever is good and perfect comes to us from God above." God loves to send perfect gifts to your children. Doesn't that encourage and comfort you?

There are conditions, though. Since God is most concerned with character, he can't bless people whose heart attitudes are wrong, no matter how he longs to. His righteous desires won't take root in rebellious hearts. That's why "The eyes of the LORD search the whole earth in order to strengthen those whose hearts are fully committed to him" (2 Chr. 16:9). God watches your children, just waiting for them to seek him with all their strength so he can bless them.

So pray for them to do their part. Ask the Lord to make them fully committed to him, to delight in him, so he can bless them and grant the desires of their hearts.

Scripture Prayers You Can Pray for Your Children

- Lord, you bless those who fear you, both great and small. May you richly bless _____ (see Ps. 115:13, 14).

- Lord God, please help _____ obey you so that he [she] will experience all these blessings (see Deut. 28:2).

- Lord, give _____ pure hands and hearts. Keep him [her] from worshiping idols and telling lies. Then he [she] will receive your blessing and have right standing with God their savior (see Ps. 24:4, 5).

- Praise you, God, the Father of our Lord Jesus Christ. You have blessed _____ with every spiritual blessing in the heavenly realms because he [she] belongs to Christ (see Eph. 1:3).

- Endow _____ with eternal blessings (see Ps. 21:6).

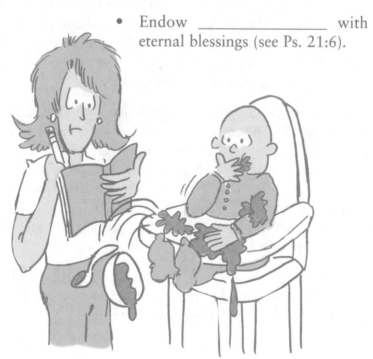

Sharing My Thoughts with the Lord in Prayer

How this applies to my family
and me

_____
_____
_____
_____
_____
_____
_____
_____
_____

My specific prayer for:

_____
_____
_____
_____
_____
_____
_____

Insights received as I prayed

_____
_____
_____
_____
_____

What I believe God will do

_____
_____
_____
_____
_____
_____

Watching for answers:

Date and answer

_____
_____
_____
_____
_____

Date and answer

_____
_____
_____
_____
_____

Date and answer

_____
_____
_____
_____

Help Them Discover
Their Gifts

Why It Is Important

In mid-June, with two publishing deadlines looming and summer chores piling up daily, I desperately needed some help around the house. My youngest son, an engineering student, had arrived home from college the day before. I knew he wouldn't mind pitching in, but (and I hate to tell you this) he's a little picky about the sort of tasks he'll do. Okay—even though this is not politically correct, I'm going to state it straight out: he hates "woman's work."

Still, even though I knew he hated housework, desperation won out, and I asked. "Hey, Tev—wanna dust the living room for me?"

Tevin pushed back from the computer, looking apologetic. "Uh—not really."

I searched my mind for a task he might deem suitable. "Weed the front flower garden?"

"Okay—sure. If you want me to."

Obviously he didn't want to do that either.

"Hey, I know! How about hauling manure from the barn?"

"Sure!" He jumped up and headed outdoors. For the next

two hours I weeded as I watched him sweat in the sun, muscles bulging, pushing wheelbarrow loads of manure past me and dumping them onto the vegetable garden. On one of his last passes, he stopped and set down the wheelbarrow. Wiping his face with the white T-shirt draped over his shoulder, he took a deep breath (Yes, I'm well aware he breathed in the aroma of cow manure) and exclaimed, "I love this. It feels great to work with my body instead of my brain for a change!"

Tevin's muscles were meant for exercise. When my son utilized his muscles for their intended purpose, he felt wonderful.

Why It Matters To You and Me

I expected hard work to exhaust my son. It energized him instead, because hauling manure allowed Tev to use his muscles for their intended purpose. In a similar way, using the spiritual gifts God gives us energizes us. It releases us to become who he created us to be. Os Guinness says, "Somehow, we human beings are never happier than when we are expressing the deepest gifts that are truly us" (as quoted in John Eldredge, *The Journey of Desire*, Thomas Nelson Publishers, 2000, page 152).

But God's gifts have a larger purpose. He gives them so we can use them to bless the body of believers. That's why it's alarming that there has been a 425-percent increase in the number of Christians who say God has not given them any gift at all. How can Christians effectively use something they don't believe they have? George Barna says:

> Imagine what might happen if nearly half of all believers had a clear and firm conviction that God has given them a supernatural ability to serve him in a specific manner. If more believers understood the nature and potential of that special empowerment, the global impact of the Christian body would be multiplied substantially.
>
> ("Awareness of Spiritual Gifts is Changing," Barna Research Online, www.barna.org, Feb. 5, 2001)

No matter how young your children are, begin praying for them to discover their gifts so they can use them in Christ's service. Ask God to fulfill their full potential.

Scripture Prayers You Can Pray for Your Children

- Heavenly Father, teach _____ that there are different kinds of spiritual gifts, but it is the same Holy Spirit who is the source of them all (see 1 Cor. 12:4).

- Thank you, Lord, for giving gifts to each of us from your great variety of spiritual gifts. Help _____ manage his [hers] well so that your generosity can flow through him [her]. If he [she] is called to be a speaker, let him [her] speak as though you yourself were speaking through him [her]. If he [she] is called to help others, let him [her] do it with all the strength and energy that you supply (see 1 Pet. 4:10, 11).

- Help _____ fan into flame the spiritual gift you gave her [him] (see 2 Tim. 1:6).

- Don't let _____ neglect the spiritual gift he [she] received (see 1 Tim. 4:14).

- O God, if you have given _____ the ability to prophesy, let her [him] speak out when she [he] has faith that you are speaking through her [him]. If her [his] gift is that of serving others, help her [him] serve them well. If she [he] is a teacher, help her [him] do a good job of teaching. If her [his] gift is to encourage others, help her [him] do it. If she [he] has money, help her [him] share it generously. If you have given her [him] leadership ability, help her [him] take the responsibility seriously. And if she [he] has a gift for showing kindness to others, help her [him] do it gladly (see Rom. 12:6–8).

Sharing My Thoughts with the Lord in Prayer

How this applies to my family and me

_____
_____
_____
_____
_____
_____
_____
_____
_____
_____

My specific prayer for:

_____
_____
_____
_____
_____
_____
_____
_____

Insights received as I prayed

_____
_____
_____
_____
_____
_____

What I believe God will do

_____
_____
_____
_____
_____
_____

Watching for answers:

Date and answer

_____
_____
_____
_____

Date and answer

_____
_____
_____
_____

Date and answer

_____
_____
_____
_____

Direct My Children to Fulfill Their Potential

Why It Is Important

I like my job. No, I love my job. There's nothing I would rather do than talk or write about the Lord, and every morning I get to sit down at the computer and share the way I think and feel about his goodness and blessings. In the afternoons I trek out to my studio to work on pastel landscapes for my gallery or draw and paint whimsical illustrations for children's books. As a friend recently said, "You're living the dream." She's right. Only this wasn't my dream. I never expected to write or create works of art.

In elementary school I hated art, because I couldn't do it. When my fourth-grade teacher assigned an illustration for each story in our reader, I refused to put crayon to paper—because my drawing looked so horrible. Artistic ability didn't surface in me until my mid-twenties, when I specifically asked for a gift from God. The very next day, while looking through a how-to-draw book for kids, I discovered I could draw a rudimentary ostrich with circles and lines. I was thrilled.

Over the years, I felt driven to develop my skill as an artist, but since I couldn't see any eternal purpose in art, I felt guilty about the waste of time and money involved. I often considered quitting, but I couldn't. Every time I would stop painting, I would feel wretched until I picked up a brush again. I didn't understand it at the time, but that drive came from God.

Eventually, I created some characters I thought would be great characters for a children's book. I asked a writer-friend to craft a story for them. She said no. So I wrote one, even though I never intended to write. I'm convinced I would never have started writing if I hadn't longed to illustrate those pumpkins. First God gave me the drive to make art; then he used my painting to draw me into writing.

Finally, he led me into the publication of my first book. After that, he even allowed me to illustrate children's books. Amazing! Still, it wasn't as fast and easy as it sounds. I faced many setbacks and discouragements along the way. At one point, when getting published felt hopeless, I had to submit my desires to him. But my friend is right. I'm living the dream—God's dream for me. It feels better than anything I might have dreamed for myself, because his plan allows me to fulfill my potential.

Why It Matters To You and Me

Your dream is probably different from mine, because God gives us each different gifts and desires. My son loves teaching college math. Just thinking about numbers makes me shudder. What fulfills me might not fulfill you. What fulfills you might not be the thing that makes your child feel complete. The good thing is that God knows what each of us needs. He knows the purpose for which he created you and your children, and "By his mighty power at work within us, he is able to accomplish infinitely more than we would ever dare to ask or hope" (Eph. 3:20).

If your son struggles with his studies, higher education may not fulfill him. If your daughter has a weak stomach, she may not be happy working in a hospital. The job that will pay the bills for your children may not gratify them, but God can fulfill them. Maybe their greatest joy will come through family, or volunteer work. More likely, God will bless them with something entirely different than you or I can imagine right now. Solomon says, "We can make our plans, but the LORD determines our steps" (Prov. 16:9). The trick is learning how to let go and let God lead. Pray for the Lord to show your children how to do that. He will enable them to experience their full potential.

Scripture Prayers You Can Pray for Your Children

- Lord, thank you for promising to guide _____ along the best pathway for her [his] life. I know you will advise and watch over her [him]. Don't let her [him] be like a senseless horse or mule that needs a bit and bridle to keep it under control (see Ps. 32:8, 9).

- I pray that _____'s heart will be flooded with light so she [he] can understand the wonderful future you have promised to those you called (see Eph. 1:18).

- Help _____ submit his [her] work to you, and then his [her] plans will succeed (see Prov. 16:3).

- I pray that you, by your power, will fulfill all _____'s good intentions and faithful deeds. Then everyone will give honor to the name of our Lord Jesus because of her [him], and she [he] will be honored along with him. This is all made possible because of the undeserved favor of our God and Lord, Jesus Christ (see 2 Thess. 1:11, 12).

- Thank you that your mighty power at work within us is able to accomplish infinitely more than we would ever dare to ask or hope (see Eph. 3:20).

- Father, I believe you will keep on guiding _____ with your counsel, leading her [him] to a glorious destiny (see Ps. 73:24).

Sharing My Thoughts with the Lord in Prayer

How this applies to my family and me

_____
_____
_____
_____
_____
_____
_____
_____
_____
_____

My specific prayer for:

_____
_____
_____
_____
_____
_____
_____

Insights received as I prayed

_____
_____
_____
_____
_____

What I believe God will do

_____
_____
_____
_____
_____
_____

Watching for answers:

Date and answer

_____
_____
_____
_____

Date and answer

_____
_____
_____
_____
_____

Date and answer

_____
_____
_____
_____

Asking God to Make My Children
Worthy of His Call on Them

Give My Children Character

Why It Is Important

In January 2003 two very different men made headlines in Oregon. Before the events that thrust them into the news, the casual observer may not have detected much difference between the two. Both were in their 30s. Both were married. Both smiled pleasantly in family photographs—but they couldn't have been more different.

One man loaded his wife and children into the family mini-van for a fun camping trip to the beach. In a snow-covered forest several miles from the ocean, the man slaughtered them and dumped their bodies beside a deserted logging road.

Two weeks later, the other man, a Coastguard rescue-swimmer, dangled from a helicopter cable in heavy winds around midnight. Shining his light on the ocean below, he spotted a survivor clinging to a life ring. The man's vacant stare told Roman he had been in the water a long time; his survival suit wouldn't protect him from the frigid water much longer. Above Roman, and almost out of fuel, the helicopter lurched in fifty-mile-per-hour winds, struggling to maneuver him close enough to snag the man. But the wind jerked Roman away every time he swung within reach.

Roman knew the helicopter, nearly out of gas, would have to fly the fifteen miles back to land to refuel soon. He felt the tug of the cable pulling him upward. It was time. Roman watched the survivor drop out of sight, into the trough of a 30-foot wave. When the man rose again, and his terror-filled gaze fixed on Roman, the rescue swimmer determined he would not leave the man alone and hopeless. Deliberately disconnecting himself from the cable, he plunged into the inky water, thus giving the helicopter permission to return to land without him.

Roman Baligad had character.

Why It Matters To You and Me

Though Roman fully expected the helicopter to leave without him, it didn't. Once in the water, he was able use his light to signal the crew where to lower the basket. With only three minutes to spare, Roman climbed aboard the helicopter with the survivor. When reporters interviewed him later, he deflected their praise to the crew.

How proud would you feel if one day your child displayed Roman's depth of character?

- Only people of character are willing to risk their lives to save others.

- Only people of character deflect praise to others.

- Only people of character refuse to take the easy way out.

- Only people of character tell the truth when a lie would make life easier.

- Only people of character stand for right when tempted to go along with the crowd.

- Only people of character refuse to complain when life buffets them.

- Only people of character remain kind when mistreated.

- Only people of character serve God when the going gets tough.

- Only people of character make society better.

Pray for God to give your children character. Then ask him to keep you from interfering when he chooses to use difficulties to perfect that character.

Scripture Prayers You Can Pray for Your Children

- Show _____ that even children are known by the way they act. May her [his] conduct be pure and right (see Prov. 20:11).

- Prompt _____ to be a wise child who accepts parental discipline (see Prov. 13:1).

- Teach _____ not to let anyone think less of him [her] because he [she] is young. Help him [her] be an example to all believers in the way he [she] lives, in his [her] love, faith, and purity (see 1 Tim. 4:12).

- Make _____ careful to live a blameless life—a life of integrity. Keep her [him] from all crooked dealings, and teach her [him] to reject perverse ideas and stay away from every evil (see Ps. 101:2–4).

- Help _____ abandon his [her] shameful ways. Make your laws all he [she] wants in life (see Ps. 119:39).

Sharing My Thoughts with the Lord in Prayer

How this applies to my family and me

_____
_____
_____
_____
_____
_____
_____
_____

My specific prayer for:

_____
_____
_____
_____
_____
_____
_____
_____

Insights received as I prayed

_____
_____
_____
_____
_____

What I believe God will do

_____
_____
_____
_____
_____

Watching for answers:

Date and answer

_____
_____
_____
_____

Date and answer

_____
_____
_____
_____

Date and answer

_____
_____
_____
_____

Make Them People of Praise

Why It Is Important

In the first chapter of Ezekiel, after a breathtaking description of the power and majesty of the winged beings surrounding God, Ezekiel describes God's throne. It looked like blue sapphire, he tells us. And "all around him was a glowing halo, like a rainbow shining through the clouds" (Ezek. 1:28). The vision so overpowered the prophet that he fell face down in the dust.

The apostle John saw God on his throne too. "The one sitting on the throne was as brilliant as gemstones—jasper and carnelian. And the glow of an emerald circled his throne like a rainbow. . . . And from the throne came flashes of lightning and the rumble of thunder" (Rev. 4:3, 5).

Daniel "watched as thrones were put in place and the Ancient One sat down to judge. . . . He sat on a fiery throne with wheels of blazing fire, and a river of fire flowed from his presence (see Dan. 7:9). Wow! Trying to visualize God's throne is mind-boggling, isn't it? The picture becomes especially astonishing if you read the chapters surrounding each of those verses.

Yet the psalmist mentions an even more startling throne. Speaking to God, he says "You are holy, enthroned in the praises of Israel" (Ps. 22:3, NKJV). Our praises are another of God's thrones! When we offer praises, he sits in the midst of them, basking in the pleasure. Can't you almost see him, face tipped up, arms out, smiling with pleasure? How incredible! Stop and think about it for a minute. The psalmist is talking about your praises. Yours! And your children's. Your praises please him that much! He longs for you to praise him. Doesn't that just blow you away?

Why It Matters To You and Me

I hate to ask what sounds like a self-serving question right in the middle of those glorious descriptions of God's throne, but—are praises only for God? Or do they benefit you and your children too? If you know God at all, you know he always gives more than he gets. If he asks you for something— and Psalms urge us over and over to offer him praise—he will bless you beyond measure if you respond.

Are you depressed? Praise the Lord. Do you feel hopeless? Offer God a sacrifice of praise even while it seems as though your problems are unsolvable. Praise him because he is sovereign. Praise him because he with you and will never leave you alone. Praise him because you know he can rescue you.

Praise is powerful. When Paul and Silas praised the Lord, a great earthquake shook the prison, and their chains fell off (see Acts 16:25, 26).

The Psalms say, "With praises from children and from tiny infants, you have built a fortress. It makes your enemies silent, and all who turn against you are left speechless" (Ps. 8:2, CEV). Praise is a show of strength. Praise silences enemies.

Praise the Lord and teach your children to praise him. If you're not quite sure how to do it, read the Psalms. I'm surprised God didn't subtitle them *A Textbook on How to Praise.* They offer all sorts of options for praising. You can: Shout, sing, tell the world how glorious God is. Tell God how awesome you think he is. Tell everyone what he has done. Clap, raise your hands, rejoice, thank him, whoop and holler, play a harp, crash cymbals together, or blow a trumpet. Make any sort of a joyful noise to him—beat on a pan with a spoon if you want to—just praise him. Praise him often. Pray for your children to develop a habit of praise. You'll be amazed at the difference it makes.

Scripture Prayers You Can Pray for Your Children

- Lord, _____ and I will praise your name! We will praise you because you are good. We will celebrate your wonderful name with music (see Ps. 135:1, 3).

- Teach _____ to shout joyful praises to you, God! Help him [her] sing about the glory of your name! Show him [her] how to tell the world how glorious you are. Your deeds are awesome! Your enemies cringe before your mighty power (see Ps. 66:1–3).

- Help _____ sing praises to you, God, our strength. Teach her [him] to sing to you, the God of Israel (see Ps. 81:1).

- Teach _____ to praise you! Show him [her] how good it is to sing praises to our God. How delightful and how right! (see Ps. 147:1).

- O God, help _____ praise your Word. Yes, Lord, teach her [him] to praise your Word (see Ps. 56:10).

Sharing My Thoughts with the Lord in Prayer

How this applies to my family and me

_____
_____
_____
_____
_____
_____
_____
_____
_____
_____

My specific prayer for:

_____
_____
_____
_____
_____
_____
_____
_____

Insights received as I prayed

_____
_____
_____
_____
_____

What I believe God will do

_____
_____
_____
_____
_____
_____

Watching for answers:

Date and answer

_____
_____
_____
_____
_____

Date and answer

_____
_____
_____
_____
_____

Date and answer

_____
_____
_____
_____

Teach Them How to Offer Grace

Why It Is Important

Tori lined up beside Kate at the starting line, arms in ready position, waiting for the gun. Today was the District meet— Tori's last race in high school, her last chance to compete at State. She had never wanted anything so badly in her life. She knew she could win. Only one girl in the field of runners stood in her way: Kate. None of the other girls was fast enough to offer a threat. If Tori could beat Kate, she would go to State. If not, Kate would go instead, and Tori's running career would be over. The problem was—Tori understood this race meant as much to Kate as it did to her.

The gun sounded. The group thundered away from the line together, but Tori and Kate quickly moved ahead of the field, running at a steady pace half a lap in front of the other girls. Tori drafted slightly behind Kate, following Coach's plan. She could hear Kate's gasping breaths. Kate sounded tired.

Tori waited until halfway through the final lap and then surged ahead of the other girl. Fixing her eyes on the finish line, she ran. Concentrating on her breathing, hoping to beat her own best time, she couldn't believe it when Kate suddenly pulled up beside her and then moved into the front position. Tori willed her legs to move faster, but she couldn't pump them any harder. It looked as if Kate would win the race, until unexpectedly, inches from the finish line, Kate pitched face forward and fell unconscious onto the track. She had pushed her body to exhaustion. The victory belonged to Tori!

But Tori refused to accept victory at that price. Hesitating only a moment, she bent down and dragged Kate over the finish line, choosing to give the win, and the opportunity to compete at State, to her competition.

Why It Matters To You and Me

Spectators watched Tori's sacrifice with awe. Because she had established her reputation as a Christian several years earlier, most understood she offered grace to Kate in order to glorify the Lord. They knew her desire to win burned hot, but she wanted to show Jesus' love more than she wanted to win.

At her final high school assembly, her coaches didn't expound on the fact that she had earned the Most Valuable Player award in four sports that year. No one mentioned the fact that coaches had dubbed her "arguably the best athlete" ever to graduate from their large high school. Instead, her non-Christian coaches chose to share stories about her character rather than tout her achievements. More than one coach fought back tears as he spoke.

Youngsters who offer grace are impressive. They impact the people around them. They show unbelievers what a true Christian should look like.

Pray for God to teach your children to put others ahead of themselves. Since it's harder to do that at home than anywhere else, pray for it to start at home. Thank God for the grace he bestows on your children every day. Ask him to continue to show his grace to them as he teaches them how to offer grace to others.

Scripture Prayers You Can Pray for Your Children

- Please pour out a spirit of grace and prayer on _____ (see Zech. 12:10).

- Lord, may your grace be with _____ (see Rom. 16:20).

- Lord God, you are _____'s light and protector. You give him [her] grace and glory. You won't withhold any good thing from him [her] if he [she] does right (see Ps. 84:11).

- Help _____ listen to what her [his] father teaches her [him]. Don't let her [him] neglect her [his] mother's teaching. Let the things she [he] learns from us crown her [him] with grace and clothe her [him] with honor (see Prov. 1:8, 9).

- Jesus, let _____ come boldly to the throne of our gracious God. There he will receive his mercy and he will find grace to help him when he needs it (see Heb. 4:16).

Sharing My Thoughts with the Lord in Prayer

How this applies to my family
and me

_____
_____
_____
_____
_____
_____
_____
_____
_____
_____
_____

My specific prayer for:

_____
_____
_____
_____
_____
_____
_____
_____

Insights received as I prayed
_____
_____
_____
_____
_____

What I believe God will do

_____
_____
_____
_____
_____
_____
_____

Watching for answers:

Date and answer

_____
_____
_____
_____
_____

Date and answer

_____
_____
_____
_____
_____

Date and answer

_____
_____
_____
_____
_____

Help Them Learn to Delay Gratification

Why It Is Important

Instant gratification: is it the cause of societal decay or a symptom of it? Opinions differ. However, most people agree that our society will sink deeper into trouble unless we learn to delay gratification. What does that mean in practical terms? Some former wife abusers on *The Oprah Show* offered an insight into that question.

Oprah Winfrey questioned one man who used to beat his wife: "How did you change?" Her voice revealed that she was impressed that the man had been able to stop hurting his wife. So was I. Men such as this don't often change. Most have had difficult childhoods and are easily hurt. Any small failure or rejection brings intense pain, because it touches old wounds that remain red and raw, though years have passed. And when the pain gets intense enough, the abuser feels relief only by inflicting physical or mental pain on another being.

"When someone hurt me, I felt relief only when I caused pain for my wife," the man said. "Punching her transferred my suffering to her and anesthetized my own pain. The times I didn't act out my anger, I suffered intense pain. When I finally determined to hold back my anger and choose to suffer rather than strike out, I got better."

"That's amazing!" Oprah interjected. "Our problems are so

different, yet that's exactly the solution I found for my eating problem. I had to be willing to suffer hunger if I wanted to lose the weight. Without the suffering I stayed heavy."

Both Oprah and the abuser, two very different people with very different problems, achieved victory through suffering. Delayed gratification requires suffering.

Why It Matters To You and Me

So many of today's "epidemics" could be wiped out if we were all willing to suffer a little.

- The epidemic of divorce wouldn't affect one million additional children each year if single adults would suffer loneliness rather than rush to marry unwisely, or if parents would choose to suffer through marriages that don't fill every need.

- The epidemics of pornography and infidelity would not exist if men and women suffered by refusing to indulge in wrong relationships that "felt right."

- The epidemic of teen pregnancy wouldn't rage through our cities and towns if young adults and teenagers would suffer by remaining abstinent until they married.

- The epidemic of obesity might not threaten the health of thousands if we would suffer mild hunger rather than overeat.

What victory doesn't require suffering? Marathon runners often "hit the wall" before finishing the race. Medical students study long hours and lose sleep in order to become doctors. Soldiers endure miserable conditions to win a war.

Jesus won the greatest victory of all time through intense suffering on the Cross. And the Bible urges us to suffer for him in return. How can we do that? I used to believe that the only people who suffered for Christ were the martyrs who endured torture for their faith, but that's incorrect. Any time we choose to obey Christ rather than fill our own needs, and it causes us to suffer, we suffer for him.

Are you working on a difficult marriage even though the easier path would be to leave? Are you doing it because you know God hates divorce? You suffer for Christ. Do you try to please God by repeatedly forgiving a coworker who backstabs you? You suffer for Christ. If you turn away from a slice of blueberry cheesecake because God has been dealing with you about exercising more self-control, you suffer for Christ.

Every time obeying God's Word temporarily makes life more difficult for you, you suffer for Christ. And you shine as an example for your children.

Pray for your children to be willing to delay gratification—to suffer—because they want to please Jesus.

Scripture Prayers You Can Pray for Your Children

- Teach _____ that if we're to share in Christ's glory, we must also share his suffering. Show her [him] that what we suffer now is nothing compared to the glory he will give us later (see Rom. 8:17, 18).

- Convince _____ that since Christ suffered physical pain, she [he] must arm herself [himself] with the same attitude that Christ had and be ready to suffer too. For if she [he] is willing to suffer for Christ, she [he] has decided to stop sinning (see 1 Pet. 4:1).

- Teach _____ that she [he] can be sure that the more she [he] suffers for Christ, the more you will shower her [him] with his comfort through Christ. So when she [he] is weighed down with troubles, it is for her [his] benefit (see 2 Cor. 1:5, 6).

- Like the apostles, help _____ rejoice if you count him [her] worthy to suffer for the name of Jesus (see Acts 5:41).

Sharing My Thoughts with the Lord in Prayer

How this applies to my family
and me

_____
_____
_____
_____
_____
_____
_____
_____
_____
_____

My specific prayer for:

_____
_____
_____
_____
_____
_____
_____

Insights received as I prayed

_____
_____
_____
_____

What I believe God will do

_____
_____
_____
_____
_____
_____

Watching for answers:

Date and answer

_____
_____
_____
_____
_____

Date and answer

_____
_____
_____
_____
_____

Date and answer

_____
_____
_____
_____

Help Them Stand Against
Wrongs in the Culture

Why It Is Important

Ann Lamott's novel Blue Shoe offers a startling glimpse into the minds of many of today's Christians. The main character in the book loves the Lord and prays without ceasing. She begs for God's help with daily problems and thanks Jesus for small blessings. Sounds wonderful, doesn't it?

The problem is that her relationship with the Lord does little to influence her morals. She experiences mild guilt after sleeping with her ex-husband, whose current wife is pregnant. She rationalizes that Jesus knows she's messed up and will forgive her. Shrugging off negative emotions, she continues the behavior. She also enjoys guilt-free sexual encounters with a boyfriend. By the end of the story, she steals another woman's husband without experiencing a tinge of remorse. The last page of the novel is filled with thoughts about the Lord, gratitude to him, and her need for him.

I want to believe that the attitudes and actions of the character in Blue Shoe bear little resemblance to people in real life who claim the name of Jesus. Unfortunately, I'm afraid many Christians are just like her.

Why It Matters To You and Me

Eighty-six percent of Americans surveyed consider themselves Christian, while sixty-eight percent of those surveyed claim a personal commitment to Jesus ("How America's Faith Has Changed Since 9/11," Barna Research Online, www.barna.org, Nov. 26, 2001). Yet, for some reason, illicit sex is widely accepted in our culture. How can our society accept immorality so easily if the majority claim to be Christian, and God condemns immorality? God's followers have ignored or forgotten the warnings in his Word. Instead of standing against the wrongs in society, they have allowed themselves to be absorbed into the declining culture. Even though God tells us to separate ourselves from the things of the world (see 2 Cor. 6:17), many Christians appear to believe they can participate in them with impunity.

This is nothing new. 2 Kings tells us of a great revival in King Josiah's day, when the entire population of Judah turned to the Lord. They promised to serve only Jehovah. They renewed Sabbath Temple worship, calling on God to bless and protect them. They looked good. They sounded righteous. They believed themselves to be godly.

They weren't.

Lured away from Jehovah, partially because of the strong pull of the illicit sex surrounding the worship of false gods, they baked cakes for the "queen of heaven" and sought after additional false gods during the week. Though God had cautioned them he couldn't tolerate such behavior, they thought everything would be fine as long as they remembered to attend services and pray to the one true God every weekend.

They were wrong. Within a few years, God was forced to destroy them.

Pray for the Lord to help your child stand firm against the culture when it opposes God's Word. Pray for your child to shine in Jesus' image and help turn our society back to the pure and undefiled worship of Jehovah and his Son, Jesus.

Scripture Prayers You Can Pray for Your Children

- I thank you that _____ will have a godly influence because he [she] is set apart for you (see 1 Cor. 7:14).

- Instruct _____ to come apart from unbelievers and separate himself [herself] from them. Don't let him [her] touch the culture's filthy things (see 2 Cor. 6:17).

- Help _____ to stop evaluating herself [himself] by what the world thinks about her [him] (see 2 Cor. 5:16).

- Jesus, you didn't ask your Father to take _____ out of the world, but to keep him [her] safe from the evil one. _____ is not part of this world any more than you were. Make _____ pure and holy by teaching him [her] your words of truth. You are sending him [her] out into the world, just as your Father sent you into the world (John 17:15–18).

- O God, I entrust _____ to you and the word of your grace. Your message is able to build him [her] up and give him [her] an inheritance with all those you have set apart for yourself (Acts 20:32).

Sharing My Thoughts with the Lord in Prayer

How this applies to my family and me

_____
_____
_____
_____
_____
_____
_____
_____
_____
_____

My specific prayer for:

_____
_____
_____
_____
_____
_____
_____

Insights received as I prayed

_____
_____
_____
_____
_____

What I believe God will do

_____
_____
_____
_____
_____
_____

Watching for answers:

Date and answer

_____
_____
_____
_____

Date and answer

_____
_____
_____
_____

Date and answer

_____
_____
_____
_____

Make Them Willing to Risk Everything for Christ

Why It Is Important

My daughter expects to be fired on Monday. Last night, while performing her duties at a live-in facility for mentally ill teenage girls, Tori flagrantly disregarded a rule. She's been called on the carpet for similar incursions before, but this violation crossed the line.

Just after ten o'clock, three clients returning from an outing staged a mutiny against the staff. Completely out of control and shrieking profanities, they quickly escalated to physical violence. Within minutes, the staff had to put three girls in lock-down.

Things quickly quieted, but frightened by the disturbance, one of the young clients curled in a fetal position on the sofa, moaning and writhing in the throes of a flashback to sexual abuse. Tori hurried to the couch and placed a hand on the girl's shoulder. "It's okay, Kisa—you're at Willow House," she told her.

Kisa opened wild, unseeing eyes. Tori leaned closer, stroking her hair and continuing in a gentle voice. "It's Tori, Kisa. You're safe here." Kisa's hysteria escalated, and Tori realized her words would never penetrate the girl's world. That's when she decided to break the prohibition of religious dialogue rule.

Very deliberately, Tori began to pray aloud. Fervently. "Dear Jesus, help Kisa . . ." Less than ten seconds into the prayer,

Kisa began to calm. Tori continued to pray with confidence, though she knew she was breaking the rules and others in the house could hear. After a few minutes, another client crept into the room, placed her hand on Kisa, and closed her eyes. Tori assumed she was praying too.

Tori knows the boss is sure to hear what happened, but she doesn't care. Kisa needs the Lord. Nothing or no one else can heal her.

Why It Matters To You and Me

Our society is a mess. Logic should dictate that leaders as well as ordinary people recognize the desperate situation, realize their solutions haven't worked, and cry out for God's help. The opposite happens. As Satan draws his thick veil of deception over our society, we turn farther from our only salvation.

It's no longer politically correct to share the Lord with hurting people. Worse, it's often against the law. Teachers are no longer allowed to pray in the classroom—not even after murderers stalk the halls shooting children. Courts have ripped the Ten Commandments out of government buildings and parks, while overcrowded prisons force the release of violent criminals.

The battle for the soul of our beloved country is already engaged and escalating. Your children must be prepared to fight, no matter what the cost. They must fight in the strength and power of the Lord. Pray for them!

Teach them to memorize scripture that will pop into their minds and uplift them when times get tough. Ask God to make them people of prayer. Pray for God to strengthen your children and make them willing to stand for him no matter how difficult things become. Pray for him to give them wisdom about when to keep silent and when to speak out. Ask the Lord to remind them that they will be victorious through him—always (see Rom. 8). Pray they won't forget that the Lord is with them, in them, that he will never leave them. Ask Jesus to make your children the beacon through which he shines to light the earth.

If you pray for your children, and in return they diligently pray and stand for righteousness, God can heal our nation.

Scripture Prayers You Can Pray for Your Children

- Remind _____ that you will bless her [him] when she [he] is mocked and persecuted and lied about, because she [he] is your follower. Teach her [him] to be happy about it, for a great reward awaits her [him] in heaven. Help her [him] remember that the ancient prophets were persecuted too (see Matt. 5:11, 12).

- Help _____ remember how much persecution and suffering the apostle Paul endured. Remind him [her] that everyone who wants to live a godly life in Christ Jesus will suffer persecution. Convince him [her] that he [she] must remain faithful to the things he [she] has been taught (see 2 Tim. 3:11–14).

- Help _____ begin to understand the incredible greatness of your power for us who believe you. This is the same mighty power that raised Christ from the dead (see Eph. 1:19).

- Give _____ a clear mind in every situation. Don't let her [him] fear suffering for you. Help her [him] work at bringing others to Christ and complete the ministry you have given her [him] (see 2 Tim. 4:5).

- Teach _____ that just as you stood with Paul and gave him strength when everyone abandoned him, you will stand by _____. Help him [her] remember that you saved Paul from certain death (2 Tim. 4:16–17).

Sharing My Thoughts with the Lord in Prayer

How this applies to my family
and me

_____
_____
_____
_____
_____
_____
_____
_____
_____
_____
_____

My specific prayer for:

_____
_____
_____
_____
_____
_____
_____
_____

Insights received as I prayed

_____
_____
_____
_____
_____
_____

What I believe God will do

_____
_____
_____
_____
_____

Watching for answers:

Date and answer

_____
_____
_____
_____

Date and answer

_____
_____
_____
_____
_____

Date and answer

_____
_____
_____
_____
_____

Praying for Godly Character

Make My Children Wise

Why It Is Important

I bumped into Vanessa as she bobbed along in the park, holding onto her Great Dane's leash, arm outstretched. She appeared her usual happy self, but after we had chatted for a while, a shadow crossed her face. "I hate getting older," she said.

"Yeah, well," I replied, smiling ruefully and rolling stiff shoulders, "I'm not too crazy about it either."

"No, I don't mean that. I hate it because now that I'm older, people assume I'm wise, so they continually dump their problems on me. I can't stand it. I wish they'd just be quiet."

Her words startled me. "You don't want to hear their problems?"

"No—it makes me feel helpless!" She spoke vehemently. "I hate listening, because there's absolutely nothing I can do to help."

"But you can help by praying," I offered. "God is real. He actually listens and reaches down to supernaturally help and comfort."

She averted her gaze. "I don't believe in that stuff. It's nothing but false hope."

Why It Matters To You and Me

Unfortunately, wisdom is not a natural outgrowth of the aging process.

Fortunately, the Bible clearly teaches us how to acquire it: "If you need wisdom—if you want to know what God wants you to do—ask him, and he will gladly tell you. He will not resent your asking" (James 1:5). It even directs us where to begin our search. "Fear of the LORD is the beginning of knowledge" (Prov. 1:7).

Better yet, we don't have to wait until we grow white hair to become wise, and neither do your children. The apostle Paul considered young Timothy wise enough to oversee a church. When Paul left for Macedonia, he asked Timothy to stay in Ephesus in order to correct the wrong doctrine promulgated by several teachers in that city. Since Paul knew the young man had the wisdom needed to deal with the situation, he urged Timothy not to let anyone look down on him because of his youth.

Where did that young man acquire so much wisdom? Timothy spent many hours studying the Scriptures and God's wisdom gleaned from his friend, the apostle Paul. Your children can learn from the same sources. Paul jotted down everything he taught Timothy. Your children can read his letters in the New Testament and then go on to study Proverbs and the rest of the Scriptures. God's wisdom is available to anyone willing to search it out.

Pray for your kids to respect the Lord enough to choose to learn about him. Pray that they will turn to the Word for the answer to every question. Ask the Lord to help them love him enough to obey him. Ask him to make them wise while they're still young.

Scripture Prayers You Can Pray for Your Children

- Don't let anyone think less of _____ because he [she] is young. Help him [her] be an example to all believers in what he [she] teaches, in the way he [she] lives, in his [her] love, his [her] faith, and his [her] purity (see 1 Tim. 4:12).

- Lord, I know wisdom will multiply _____'s days and add years to her [his] life. Help her [him] become wise. She [He] will be the one to benefit. Don't let her [him] scorn wisdom and suffer (see Prov. 9:11, 12).

- Teach _____ to choose your instruction rather than silver, and knowledge over pure gold. For wisdom is far more valuable than rubies. Nothing my child desires can be compared with it (see Prov. 8:10, 11).

- Make _____ a wise man [woman], mightier than a strong man [woman]. Make him [her] a man [woman] of knowledge, more powerful than a strong man [woman] (see Prov. 24:5).

- Lord, you grant wisdom. Make _____ godly so you can grant her [him] a treasure of good sense. Let knowledge and understanding come from her [his] mouth. Help her [him] understand what is right, just, and fair, and how to find the right course of action every time. Let wisdom enter her [his] heart and knowledge fill her [him] with joy. Allow wise planning to watch over her [him] and understanding to keep her [him] safe. Let wisdom save her [him] from evil people (see Prov. 2:6–12).

Sharing My Thoughts with the Lord in Prayer

How this applies to my family and me

_____
_____
_____
_____
_____
_____
_____
_____
_____
_____

My specific prayer for:

_____
_____
_____
_____
_____
_____
_____

Insights received as I prayed

_____
_____
_____
_____

What I believe God will do

_____
_____
_____
_____
_____
_____

Watching for answers:

Date and answer

_____
_____
_____

Date and answer

_____
_____
_____

Date and answer

_____
_____
_____

Help Them Believe in Absolute Truth

Why It Is Important

A large Christian publisher recently sent me a children's novel to edit. I read it and then flipped to the "Helps for Readers" section at the end of the book. The first two sentences on that page shook me to the core. They said: "The Ten Commandments aren't a list of rules that we have to follow or else. Rather, they're ten ideas that show us what is important to God."

I couldn't believe it. It reminded me of the joke about the Ten Commandments really being the "Ten Suggestions"—only this author wasn't kidding. When did God's Commandments stop being rules and become ideas? God considered his commandments so urgent that he spoke them to the Israelites "face to face from the heart of the fire on the mountain" (Deut. 5:4). Then he wrote them with his own hand on stone tablets so they would never forget his exact words. Jesus obeyed all ten, taking special care to set the Pharisees straight about the Sabbath law, which they had twisted.

This Christian author was telling impressionable children something false and dangerous. Why would she do that? I'm quite certain she intended no harm. Rather, I believe her to be the product of a society that no longer understands or believes in absolute truth.

Why It Matters To You and Me

Studies conducted by the Barna Research Group of Ventura, California, found that sixty-four percent of adults surveyed say truth is always relative to the person and the situation. Eighty-six percent of teenagers surveyed say moral truth is not absolute. But the most shocking statistic concerns born-again Christians: only one out of three now believes in absolute moral truth ("Americans are Most Likely to Base Truth on Feelings," Barna Research Online, www.barna.org, Feb. 12, 2002).

George Barna defines absolute truth this way, "God has communicated a series of moral principles in the Bible that are meant to be the basis of our thoughts and actions, regardless of our preferences, feelings or situation." He continues: "The virtual disappearance of this cornerstone of the Christian faith is probably the best indicator of the waning strength of the Christian Church in America today." (Barna, "Americans are Most Likely. . . .")

Born-again parents who don't have a firm grip on and belief in the concept of absolute truth are bound to pass false beliefs along to their children—even though they love their children and mean well, just like the author above.

If we want society to survive and thrive, we must accept God's Word as absolute truth. Without a belief in absolute truth, society has nothing on which to base laws and rules. Without absolute truth, who is to say abortion, adultery, and stealing are wrong? Without God's truth, people don't recognize sinful, detestable things as bad. Without absolute truth, societies degenerate.

We must pray for our children to embrace absolute truth if we care about their souls. Pray for your children to employ the Bible rather than feelings, or what other people think and do, as a basis for deciding right and wrong. Ask God to keep the people who teach and write for them on the right track. Pray that your children will influence rather than be influenced. Pray for them to be part of God's army, standing strong in his truth, helping restore our nation to righteousness.

Scripture Prayers You Can Pray for Your Children

- Lord, help _____ believe that your decrees are perfect; they are entirely worthy of our trust; your promises have been thoroughly tested; your justice is eternal, and your law is perfectly true (see Ps. 119:138, 140, 142).

- Jesus, show _____ that if he [she] keeps obeying your teachings, he [she] will know the truth, and the truth will set him [her] free (see John 8:31, 32).

- Jesus, you are the way, the truth, and the life. No one can come to the Father except through you (see John 14:6).

- Help _____ know that though everyone else in the world may be liars, you are true (see Rom. 3:4).

- Urge _____ to defend the truth of the Good News. You gave this truth once for all time to your holy people (see Jude 3).

Sharing My Thoughts with the Lord in Prayer

How this applies to my family
and me

_____
_____
_____
_____
_____
_____
_____
_____
_____
_____
_____

My specific prayer for:

_____
_____
_____
_____
_____
_____
_____

Insights received as I prayed

_____
_____
_____
_____
_____

What I believe God will do

_____
_____
_____
_____
_____
_____

Watching for answers:

Date and answer

_____
_____
_____
_____

Date and answer

_____
_____
_____
_____

Date and answer

_____
_____
_____
_____

Teach Them the Importance of Obedience

Why It Is Important

Recently my husband and I traveled to a university town to buy a house. A beautiful young woman answered the door of the home we hoped to purchase. Worship music played in the background while she graciously showed us through the tastefully decorated rooms. Not only was she charming and sweet, but as we talked it appeared obvious to us that she was a Christian. I felt warm affection for her. Then she said something that shocked me.

"My boyfriend and I have lived here for the last two years." It was apparent they had a sexual relationship, yet she felt no hesitancy about telling us, even though the Bible makes it clear that God forbids sex outside of marriage, plus she knew we were Christians. I left the house and cried. I still pray for her.

At church a few weeks later, I stopped to hug an old acquaintance. Her son is my oldest son's age. Her ex-husband once taught two of my children in Sunday school. When I inquired about her boy, she informed me he was living with his girlfriend. "Oh, I'm so sorry," I told her. "You must be heartbroken."

She shrugged. "I guess I can't be too upset. I'm living with my boyfriend." She considers herself a Christian, a God-seeker, yet she seemed to feel no shame about disobeying God's commands. She casually chatted about her sin—in God's house!

Why It Matters To You and Me

Somehow we Christians twist the concept of freedom in Christ to mean we can do anything we want to and everything will be just fine. We buy into the "if it feels good do it" philosophy—because we know God will forgive anything. He'll forgive sex outside of marriage; he'll forgive lies; he'll forgive cruelty.

While that's true, it isn't the point. He longs for us to love him, and his Word says we show our love for him by obeying his commands.

The Old Testament exhorts us, "Be careful to obey all the commands I give you; show love to the LORD your God by walking in his ways and clinging to him" (Deut. 11:22). In the New Testament, Jesus pleads for us to show our love through obedience: "I have loved you even as the Father has loved me. Remain in my love. When you obey me, you remain in my love, just as I obey my Father and remain in his love" (John 15:9, 10). "If you love me, obey my commandments" (John 14:15).

I'm certain that both of the women mentioned above believe they love God. Yet they both flagrantly disobey him. Do you think he feels loved by them?

All disobedience causes the Lord grief. Not only is sexual sin an abomination to God—lies are unacceptable too. So are greed, gossiping, quarreling, thinking impure or hostile thoughts—the list is long. We indulge ourselves without thinking how it hurts our Lord. It's easy to fall into sin. Obeying God is not always easy, but the Holy Spirit working through us gives us power to overcome the sinful nature.

I know you want your children to love Jesus. Pray for them to make him feel loved—by obeying him.

Scripture Prayers You Can Pray for Your Children

- Lord God, you commanded _____ to obey all your laws and to fear you for his [her] own prosperity and well-being. Show him [her] that he [she] is righteous when he [she] obeys all the commands you have given him [her] (see Deut. 6:24, 25).

- Convince _____ to choose to love you, obey you, and commit herself [himself] to you, for you are her life. Then she [he] will live long in the land (see Deut. 30:20).

- Teach _____ to fear you and to obey your commands, for this is the duty of every person. Make him [her] understand that you will judge us for everything we do, including every secret thing, whether good or bad (see Eccles. 12:13, 14).

- Show _____ that she [he] can be sure she [he] belongs to you by obeying your commandments. Teach her [him] that if someone says he or she belongs to you but doesn't obey your commandments, that person is a liar and does not live in truth. Show her [him] that those who obey your Word really do love you. That's the way she [he] will know whether or not she [he] lives in you (see 1 John 2:3–5).

- Teach _____ that even though Jesus was your Son, he learned obedience from the things he suffered. In this way, you qualified him as a perfect high priest, and he became the source of eternal salvation for all those who obey him (see Heb. 5:8, 9).

Sharing My Thoughts with the Lord in Prayer

How this applies to my family and me

_____
_____
_____
_____
_____
_____
_____
_____
_____
_____

My specific prayer for:

_____
_____
_____
_____
_____
_____
_____
_____

Insights received as I prayed

_____
_____
_____
_____
_____

What I believe God will do

_____
_____
_____
_____
_____

Watching for answers:

Date and answer

_____
_____
_____

Date and answer

_____
_____
_____
_____

Date and answer

_____
_____
_____
_____

Make Them Kind and Considerate

Why It Is Important

I breezed through most of my first pregnancy teaching social studies and literature to junior high kids in Yamhill, Oregon. Up through my first six months, I jogged around the track with my students after school. I would do three eight-minute miles, finish up with dry heaves, and feel energized for the drive home.

Life took a downturn in my seventh month. A week before school ended for the summer, the weather turned hot. That particular spring set an all-time Oregon heat record that still hasn't been broken. The hot weather drained my strength. I could barely breathe. I dragged myself around the classroom most afternoons, struggling to keep my eyes open. I vividly remember my last-period social studies class when I decided it would be acceptable for the students to take turns reading aloud from their books, just this once.

After a few minutes, I decided it would be okay for me to sit down at my desk . . . just this once. I wouldn't . . . close my eyes . . . or anything. . . .

In my defense, I don't think I slept very long. When I woke up, the room was completely silent except for a single male voice reading something about Vermont. When he finished his paragraph, another student took up where he left off. That's about the time they noticed my eyes were open. I know because the reader stopped and several students suddenly glanced at me with concern. There was a long pause before one girl whispered, "It's okay, Mrs. Taylor. We've got it. You can go back to sleep." The rest of the class nodded in agreement.

I don't think I've ever felt more loved.

Why It Matters To You and Me

What a golden opportunity my students missed! They could have gone wild. It happens. I once met a teacher whose sixth-graders scribbled on her with permanent markers. I've seen more than one teacher leave a classroom in tears due to the rude behavior of their students.

What an incredible group of children I had! How amazing that they would choose to treat me with thoughtfulness! To this day I swell with pride when I think of them. I'll always remember that class with fondness.

That's the effect considerate people usually have on us—we remember them, love them, want to treat them nicely to return their kindness, want to be like them.

I know you want your children to be thoughtful. That's why you teach them manners and admonish them to treat each other well. The thing is, true kindness comes from the heart. So along with all the parenting and teaching, you need to pray for God to fill their hearts with his goodness and love. Ask his Holy Spirit to control their lives. If they let him do that, thoughtfulness, kindness, and goodness will gush from them to bless others.

Scripture Prayers You Can Pray for Your Children

- Lord, never let loyalty and kindness get away from _____. Teach her [him] to wear them like a necklace and write them deep within her [his] heart. Then she [he] will find favor with both you and people, and she [he] will gain a good reputation (see Prov. 3:3, 4).

- Jesus, may your Holy Spirit control _____'s life. Produce this kind of fruit in him [her]: love, joy, peace, patience, kindness, goodness, faithfulness, gentleness, and self-control (see Gal. 5:22, 23).

- Help _____ love others with genuine affection, and take delight in honoring them (see Rom. 12:10).

- Lord, _____ has been called to live in freedom—not freedom to satisfy her [his] sinful nature, but freedom to serve others in love. So help her [him] to love her [his] neighbor as herself [himself] (see Gal. 5:13, 14).

- Help _____ do for others what he [she] would like them to do for him [her]. That is a summary of all that is taught in the law and the prophets (see Matt. 7:12).

- Make _____ gentle, a person who shows true humility to everyone (see Titus 3:2).

Sharing My Thoughts with the Lord in Prayer

How this applies to my family and me

_____
_____
_____
_____
_____
_____
_____
_____
_____

My specific prayer for:

_____
_____
_____
_____
_____
_____

Insights received as I prayed

_____
_____
_____
_____
_____

What I believe God will do

_____
_____
_____
_____
_____

Watching for answers:

Date and answer

_____
_____
_____

Date and answer

_____
_____
_____

Date and answer

_____
_____
_____

Fill Them with Gratitude

Why It Is Important

In the thirty-eighth chapter of Job, God asks several mind-boggling questions. "Do you know the location of the gates of death?" he asks Job. "What supports the foundations of the earth?" And then—boom! He makes a mundane statement about water and ice. It's not even a question, just boring words about something ordinary.

Or is it? Water changing to something solid might seem quite extraordinary to me if I had never seen ice before. Water has no shape. It moves. I can't grasp it. If I rest a pebble on its surface, it falls right through. Yet God figured out how to make water solid like a rock. The frozen surface of a lake not only holds up a pebble but can also be strong enough to support a semi truck. If water and ice seem ordinary to me, it's because I take God and his miracles for granted.

Isn't that sad? God wants to be appreciated, and I take him for granted. I get so accustomed to the miracles all around me that I barely notice them. God is the one who locked the sea into place so it wouldn't overrun our homes. He keeps the sun shining and sends the rain. It doesn't just happen. He's the one who stores molten fire deep in the earth and hides fire in the form of lightning in the clouds. I get so used to all his wonders and the blessings he sends my way that I forget to tell him how much I appreciate them. And he wants to hear it.

Why It Matters To You and Me

Does it surprise you that God wants our gratitude? Exodus 20 tells us right out that he is a jealous God who doesn't want to share our affections with anyone or anything. Over and over throughout the Bible, he tells us he loves us deeply. He loves us so much he gave his own Son for us.

You long to hear that the people you love appreciate all you do for them, don't you? God wants the same thing. We're made in his image, you know. The emotions we experience come from him. That should help us understand him.

Are you better at saying thank you than I am? I hope so. Because you're the example your children will follow. If you're someone who continually thanks the Lord, your children probably will too.

And here's another piece of good news about gratitude: It does more than please God. If your children thank the Lord, it will benefit their emotional health. Philippians 4:6, 7 says if you "tell God what you need, and thank him for all he has done . . . you will experience God's peace, which is far more wonderful than the human mind can understand."

Do you want your children to be contented and peaceful? Pray for God to fill their hearts with thanksgiving.

Scripture Prayers You Can Pray for Your Children

- God, your want our true thanks. Teach _____ to give her [his] true thanks to you (see Ps. 50:14).

- Lord, call _____ to give thanks to you and to sing praises to you, the Most High. It is good to do that (see Ps. 92:1).

- No matter what happens, always make _____ thankful, for this is your will for him [her] because he [she] belongs to Christ Jesus" (see 1 Thess. 5:18).

- The angels said, "Blessing and glory and wisdom and thanksgiving and honor and power and strength belong to our God forever and forever. Amen!" So teach _____ to continually thank you (see Rev. 7:12).

- Let _____'s life overflow with thanksgiving for all you have done (see Col. 2:7).

Sharing My Thoughts with the Lord in Prayer

How this applies to my family and me

_____
_____
_____
_____
_____
_____
_____
_____
_____
_____

My specific prayer for:

_____
_____
_____
_____
_____
_____
_____

Insights received as I prayed

_____
_____
_____
_____
_____

What I believe God will do

_____
_____
_____
_____
_____
_____

Watching for answers:

Date and answer

_____
_____
_____
_____
_____

Date and answer

_____
_____
_____
_____
_____

Date and answer

_____
_____
_____
_____
_____

Give Them a Strong
Work Ethic

Why It Is Important

I first glimpsed a startling new trend sweeping our nation about ten years ago. When a friend's daughter graduated from college, I assumed she would immediately pursue the career on which she had spent thousands of dollars and countless hours. Instead, she found a part-time job in a nursing home working ten hours a week. "I don't need to work any more than that," she told her mother. "All I want is enough money to pay expenses so I have time to enjoy life."

Since then, I have seen young people across the country behaving in a similar manner.

- Geoff applied for food stamps rather than work to support himself while earning his graduate degree.

- When Megan's mother told her to look for work and start supporting herself, Megan balked. It was more important to spend time with friends, she said.

- Instead of saving money to provide for his needs, Beau quit full-time employment and then mailed out a letter asking acquaintances to send him money for a short-term mission trip.

Many Christian young people today value enjoying life and ministering to others but view work as unnecessary. That's not the perspective the apostle Paul took in the Bible. The consummate missionary, he supported himself as a tentmaker while he spread the gospel across the ancient world and wrote much of the New Testament (see Acts 18:3).

He took a strong stance on the importance of work, commanding the early believers, "Stay away from any Christian who lives in idleness and doesn't follow the tradition of hard work we gave you" (2 Thess. 3:6). Then he established a firm rule: "Whoever does not work should not eat" (v. 10). He addressed his strongest words to people who refused to work for their own families: "Those who won't care for their own relatives, especially those living in the same household, have denied what we believe. Such people are worse than unbelievers" (1 Tim. 5:8).

Why It Matters To You and Me

I believe the Great Commission centers around work. Greek scholars tell us that Jesus' words in Matthew 28:19 should be translated, "As you go, make disciples of all nations." In other words, as we go about our daily work, we will have opportunities to meet and interact with people. Work is the vehicle that puts us in contact with nonbelievers. Our godly actions as well as our words will witness to non-Christians as they observe our day-to-day work behavior. This is one way we ordinary people can do our part in winning the world for the Lord. Non-believers will see Christ in us and want what we have.

If we know that and we see the upcoming generation's tendency to shy away from work, shouldn't we pray for our children to learn how to work—and work hard? Paul commands, "Work with enthusiasm, as though you were working for the Lord rather than for people" (Eph. 6:7).

While they're young, begin asking God to show them how important work is to him. Ask him to help them enjoy work.

Scripture Prayers You Can Pray for Your Children

- Please keep _____ from living an idle life, refusing to work and wasting time meddling in other people's business. In the name of Jesus Christ, I pray for him [her] to settle down and get to work to earn his [her] own living (see 2 Thess. 3:11, 12).

- Please keep _____ from laziness and considering herself [himself] smarter than seven wise counselors (see Prov. 26:16).

- Teach _____ a lesson from the ants. Help him [her] learn from the ants' ways and be wise! Even though they have no prince, governor, or ruler to make them work, they labor hard all summer, gathering food for the winter. Teach _____ this lesson: A little extra sleep, a little more slumber, a little folding of the hands to rest—and poverty will pounce on him [her] like a bandit, and scarcity will attack him [her] like an armed robber. (see Prov. 6:6–11).

- Let _____'s light so shine before everyone, that they may see his [her] good works and glorify you, our Father in heaven (see Matt. 5:16, NKJV).

- Help _____ to follow your rules for doing your work, just as an athlete either follows the rules or is disqualified and wins no prize (see 2 Tim. 2:5).

Sharing My Thoughts with the Lord in Prayer

How this applies to my family and me

_____
_____
_____
_____
_____
_____
_____
_____
_____

My specific prayer for:

_____
_____
_____
_____
_____
_____
_____

Insights received as I prayed

_____
_____
_____
_____
_____
_____

What I believe God will do

_____
_____
_____
_____
_____

Watching for answers:

Date and answer

_____
_____
_____
_____

Date and answer

_____
_____
_____
_____

Date and answer

_____
_____
_____
_____

Asking God to Establish Them in Him

Be Their Sure Foundation

Why It Is Important

Cherise and I taught school together and then retired to raise our families. Busy with young children, we rarely had time for each other the way we used to, but we did chat via telephone every couple of weeks. That's how she happened to tell me about it. "Friday night I'm going out with friends to see a male stripper."

I nearly choked. "What?"

Her voice took on an uncertain tone. "You think I shouldn't go?"

"Absolutely—don't do it! There's no question it would be wrong."

"Really? It didn't feel right to me either, but Joyce and Sherry made me feel kind of silly about it. They go all the time, and they say there's nothing wrong with it. It's just a fun night out with the girls."

Since my friend's parents had failed to teach her God's Word, she had no foundation from which to operate. Sorting out right from wrong was difficult for her. When women she trusted insisted that watching a male stripper was harmless, she had no yardstick by which to evaluate their claims.

Why It Matters To You and Me

Fortunately, my friend was a new Christian who desired to do the right thing. After I explained what the Bible says about keeping her thoughts pure, she declined to participate in something she now understood as wrong. Through studying the Word and learning about Jesus from friends, she is now laying the foundation her parents neglected.

Jesus taught about building on a sure foundation: "Anyone who listens to my teaching and obeys me is wise, like a person who builds a house on solid rock. Though the rain comes in torrents and the floodwaters rise and the winds beat against that house, it won't collapse, because it is built on rock. But anyone who hears my teaching and ignores it is foolish, like a person who builds a house on sand. When the rains and floods come and the winds beat against that house, it will fall with a mighty crash" (Matt. 7:24–27).

The foundation you build for your children by teaching them to cherish God and his laws will not only spare them from many potentially damaging mistakes—it will also keep them from collapsing in tough times. Haven't you heard Christians going through loss exclaim, "I don't see how anyone could possibly get through something like this without the Lord!" How many times have you felt that way yourself?

Satan will tempt your children. Crises will arise in their lives. There's nothing you can do to prevent it. But you can help them build a sure foundation so they can live victoriously through every problem they face.

Pray for them to remember God's laws and obey the Lord. Pray for them to turn to him the moment trouble raises its ugly head. If they do, they won't collapse. That's a promise.

Scripture Prayers You Can Pray for Your Children

- Lord, though disaster strikes like a cyclone, whirling the wicked away, make _____ godly so that he [she] will have a lasting foundation (see Prov. 10:25).

- O God, you established Jesus as our firm foundation stone. He is a firm foundation, a tested and precious cornerstone that is safe to build on. Help _____ believe so she [he] need never run away again (see Isa. 28:16).

- Let _____ be like a person who builds a house on a strong foundation laid upon the underlying rock. When the floodwaters rise and break against the house, it stands firm because it is well built (see Luke 6:48).

- Heavenly Father, no one can lay any other foundation than the one we already have—Jesus Christ (see 1 Cor. 3:11). Help _____ understand and believe that.

- Lord, thank you that _____ is a stone in your house, built on the foundation of the apostles and the prophets. And the cornerstone is Christ Jesus himself (see Eph. 2:20).

Sharing My Thoughts with the Lord in Prayer

How this applies to my family
and me

_____
_____
_____
_____
_____
_____
_____
_____
_____
_____

My specific prayer for:

_____
_____
_____
_____
_____
_____
_____
_____

Insights received as I prayed

_____
_____
_____
_____
_____

What I believe God will do

_____
_____
_____
_____
_____
_____

Watching for answers:

Date and answer

_____
_____
_____
_____
_____

Date and answer

_____
_____
_____
_____
_____

Date and answer

_____
_____
_____
_____
_____

Teach Them to Treasure Your Word

Why It Is Important

Are you the perfect parent? I'm afraid I haven't been. I did my best, though. I would never have been one of those mothers in the news who leaves her baby in the car while she dashes into the convenience store "just for a second." Not me.

Not a chance. I always laboriously unbuckled all three of my children and took them in with me, even if I could see them through the big plate-glass window the whole time, even on a miserable, rainy Oregon day. I treasured my children too much to ever compromise their safety.

Still, I made mistakes. Lots of them.

I did one thing right, though. Because I knew how flawed I am, I told my children: "I make mistakes, but God doesn't. His Word is always right. So if you ever disagree with a rule or something I do, read the Bible until you find out what God says about the issue. If you can show me where God's Word says I'm wrong—you win. Hands down. Instantly." I told them that at a very young age. I repeated it over and over as they matured.

I wanted them to learn early that God has all the answers. He's never wrong, and he's their final authority. I would gradually parent them less and less, while God would be their Father for all eternity.

Why It Matters To You and Me

For years I've read a minimum of three chapters from the Bible every morning. I still do it. Each time I read, I ask the Lord to give me a fresh insight. I long for wisdom, and I know I'll get it from God's Word. I've always tried to pass that wisdom along to my children,but—and here's that same old problem again—I'm imperfect. No matter how hard I try or how pure my motives, I'm not infallible. And neither is anyone else. Not even the pastor. We all have the potential to misunderstand God's words. We all mess up.

That's why I always prayed for my children to treasure God's Word and develop a habit of reading the Bible themselves. No matter how old they get, as long as they study God's Word and listen to the Holy Spirit as they read it, God can keep working on them, perfecting them.

My children are all in their early twenties now. My time to parent them is over—and I miss it terribly. But because they are all dedicated to reading the Bible, I don't worry about them as much. (Notice I said, "as much." Moms never quite give up wanting to mother. And mothers tend to worry—at least we imperfect ones do.) I know God will convict them anytime they start to stray from his path. He loves them even more than I do. He knows what's best for them. His Word is sharper than a two-edged sword, and I'm so grateful for that.

Pray for your children to love God's Word, to actually enjoy reading it, and to cling to it whenever they need comfort or answers.

Scripture Prayers You Can Pray for Your Children

- O Lord, teach _____ that your Word stands firm in heaven forever. Your faithfulness, which extends to him [her], is as enduring as the earth you created. Show him [her] that your laws remain true today, for everything serves your plans (see Ps. 119:89–91).

- Use your commandments to give _____ understanding; let her [him] hate every false way of life. Your Word is a lamp for her [his] feet and a light for her [his] path (see Ps. 119:104, 105).

- Teach _____ to rejoice in your Word like one who finds a great treasure (see Ps. 119:162).

- Let your words sustain _____, just as they did Jeremiah. Let them bring him [her] great joy and become his [her] heart's delight, for he [she] bears your name, O Lord God Almighty (see Jer. 15:16).

- Lord, _____ has been taught the holy Scriptures from childhood, and they have given him [her] the wisdom to receive the salvation that comes by trusting in Christ Jesus. Thank you that all Scripture is inspired by you and is useful to teach him [her] what is true and to make him [her] realize what is wrong in his [her] life. It will straighten him [her] out and teach him [her] to do what is right (see 2 Tim. 3:15, 16).

Sharing My Thoughts with the Lord in Prayer

How this applies to my family
and me

_____
_____
_____
_____
_____
_____
_____
_____
_____
_____

My specific prayer for:

_____
_____
_____
_____
_____
_____
_____
_____

Insights received as I prayed

_____
_____
_____
_____
_____

What I believe God will do

_____
_____
_____
_____
_____
_____
_____

Watching for answers:

Date and answer

_____
_____
_____
_____
_____

Date and answer

_____
_____
_____
_____
_____
_____

Date and answer

_____
_____
_____
_____
_____